A Tour on
THE UNDERGROUND
RAILROAD
along
THE OHIO RIVER

To Vic & Doug —
Hope we can meet
along the tour sometime
soon!

Nancy Spears Theiss

A Tour on THE UNDERGROUND RAILROAD *along* THE OHIO RIVER

Nancy Stearns Theiss

THE
History
PRESS

Published by The History Press
Charleston, SC
www.historypress.com

Copyright © 2020 by Nancy Stearns Theiss
All rights reserved

Front cover, right: Louisville waterfront sketch. *University of Louisville Archives Special Collections Digital Collections.*

First published 2020

Manufactured in the United States

ISBN 9781467143752

Library of Congress Control Number: 2019951837

CONTENTS

PREFACE

In 2005, the Oldham County History Center launched a research program to explore the sites that were described by native son Henry Bibb (1814–1854). His narrative, published in 1849, *The Life and Adventures of Henry Bibb: An American Slave*, was an essential part of the Underground Railroad movement. I discovered Bibb when I was doing research for an African American exhibit in our museum. Bibb was well known among academic circles, but for me, who grew up in Oldham County, Kentucky, his name was unknown.

Reading his narrative for the first time was difficult. As he described his life in the community where I grew up, I was horrified, sad and angry. It was upsetting for me to think that we had never lifted this man up in his native home. The acts of inhumanity and torture directed toward him; his wife, Malinda; and daughter, Mary Frances, from slaveholders were unthinkable within the context of a community where I was raised.

At the time that we began to recognize Bibb's contributions in our history center, there was a lot of activity in our region regarding the Underground Railroad (UGRR). In 1998, the National Park Service launched a new program, the National Underground Railroad Network, that encouraged local groups to research local sites and nominate them for membership in the network. The criteria being that the site must be either a place of escape for a freedom seeker or a place of refuge. This corresponded with a large effort in Cincinnati to raise funds for a new museum, the National Underground Railroad Freedom Center, which was prominently built on the Ohio River waterfront between the Bengals and Reds stadiums. For a featured exhibit, a slave pen jail, built and owned by John Anderson from Mason County, Kentucky, had been moved from Mason County and was reconstructed at the National Underground Railroad Freedom Center.

The program that the Oldham County History Center began on Bibb in 2005 included some experts in slave history, such as Diane Coon, a local researcher who had been working to identify UGRR conductors and stations along the Indiana borders. Carl Westmoreland, a historian from the National Underground Freedom Center in the research and placement of the Anderson Slave Jail from Mason County to Cincinnati, also attended that first meeting.

The most critical person for our research and studies from that first gathering in 2005 has been archaeologist Jeannine Kreinbrink. Jeannine was the lead archaeologist for the deconstruction and reconstruction of the Anderson Slave Jail at the Freedom Center. Her critical work gave context to the lives of those enslaved in Anderson's jail and provides insight to the daily activities that would have occurred between the Anderson family and those gathered and chained as slaves for shipment to the larger slave markets.

We began a partnership with Jeannine and her associate, Doug VonStroh, to conduct archaeological programs identified from our group research as the Bibb Escapes/William Gatewood Plantation. The site, now on the National Park Service National Underground Railroad Network, is where Bibb, Malinda and Mary Frances were enslaved by William Gatewood. Gatewood was a justice of the peace and state representative for Oldham County when the county was first organized in 1824. This site, outside of Bedford, Kentucky, was part of Oldham County until 1836, when boundary lines were redrawn to form Trimble County.

The Bibb Escapes/Gatewood Plantation site is on private property owned by World War II veteran Colonel Glen Fisher. A native of Trimble County, Colonel Fisher has very generously given permission for the Oldham County Historical Society to conduct archaeology programs at the Gatewood site where Bibb and his family lived until they escaped, were recaptured and were sold down the river to the New Orleans slave markets. In his time on German occupied battlefields during World War II, Colonel Fisher witnessed and experienced the sacrifices for freedom. His generosity has provided opportunities for hundreds of students and families to participate in archaeology programs conducted under the guidance of Jeannine and Doug. In 2007, we began our first dig, and with support of our board of directors and members of the Oldham County

Archaeologist Jeannine Kreinbrink with students at the summer field study on the Bibb Escapes/Gatewood plantation site. *Author's collection.*

Historical Society, we have had four public digs and an annual field study for high school students each year.

In 2016, we were recognized by the National Park Service for adding two sites to the National Underground Railroad Network: the Bibb Escapes/ Gatewood Plantation and the J.C. Barnett Library and Archives. We now offer National Park Service passport stamps for visitors. The Barnett Library and Archives are part of our Oldham County History Center campus and contain many slave court documents, including escapes, ownership papers and court cases. The Barnett Library and Archives was the home of James and Amanda Mount around 1840. In 2004, Lucretia Davenport donated a collection of items that belonged to Amanda Mount (1814–1888) and were passed down through the Mount family. The papers included runaway ads (placed by James Mount, who served as jailor at the time), family slave ownership papers, bounty hunter ads and personal family letters describing slaveholdings, sells and deeds.

When we had our ceremony to dedicate our Bibb site and Mount House to the National Park Service, I had the opportunity to meet Dr.

In 2016 the Oldham County Historical Society received two designations on the National Park Service National UGRR Network. (*Left to right*) Dr. Afua Cooper and Sheri Jackson with National Park Service. *Author's collection.*

Afua Cooper, who was our invited guest for the induction ceremony. Dr. Cooper is the James Robinson Johnston Chair of Black Canadian Studies at Dalhousie University in Nova Scotia and the founder of the Black Canadian Studies Association. Dr. Cooper's dissertation was titled "Doing Battle in Freedom's Cause: Henry Bibb, Abolitionism, Race Uplift, and Black Manhood, 1842–1854" (2000). Afua's research on Bibb, along with her personal experiences as a native Jamaican, where reggae culture embraces heritage, supported our efforts to uplift our own heritage at the Oldham County History Center.

Since the National Park Service created the National Underground Railroad Network in 1998, there has been a waterfall of research, books, exhibits and programs on the topic. With the establishment of the Main Street Programs by the National Trust for Historic Preservation in 1980, towns along the Ohio River have created historic districts, preserving and protecting these pioneer towns that were centers of commerce and trade in the nineteenth century. In 2018, the Oldham County History Center organized a three-day Underground Railroad bus tour that began in LaGrange, Kentucky and toured the Ohio River. The tour emphasized the associations of sites with the conductors of the UGRR. The tour connected the dots from town to town and routes of escape.

The story of the UGRR along the Ohio River is quite remarkable. You have a slave state, Kentucky, where the river provides 664 miles of opportunity for freedom seekers. As the steamboat era developed and traffic increased, conductors, fugitives and slave catchers lined up along the bank, often using steamboats, canals and railways for escape and capture.

Sites in this book were chosen based on detailed documented, and many were repeated through narratives of conductors, like Levi Coffin; fugitive slaves, like Henry Bibb; and novelists, like Harriet Beecher Stowe.

ACKNOWLEDGEMENTS

I would like to thank John Rodrigue, editor for The History Press, for his help and suggestions on this project. His input and interest were very much appreciated. A very special thanks to copyeditor Hayley Behal for her review.

Thanks, as always, to my best friend and husband of many years, Jim Theiss, who is my backup for images, for reading my work and offering helpful suggestions.

The following people gave me a lot of support, time, information and enthusiasm for this project:

Pam Fields, office manager—Oldham County Historical Society
Helen Fields, genealogist, author and educator—Oldham County Historical Society
Jeannine Kreinbrink—K & V Cultural Resources Management
John VonStrohe—K & V Cultural Resources Management
Colonel Glenn Fisher—Bibb Escapes/Gatewood Plantation
Afua Cooper, PhD, associate professor, James Robinson Johnston Chair in Black Canadian Studies—Dalhousie University
Hillary Delaney and Bridgett Striker—Boone County Public Library
Christina Hartleib—Harriet Beecher Stowe House
Jan Vetrus—Eleutherian College Incorporated
John Nyberg—Jefferson County Historical Society
Keith Norrington—Howard Steamboat Museum

Travis C. Vasconcelos—Howard Steamboat Museum

Pam Venard, local historian, Trimble County area

Pam Peters, historian and author, New Albany

Tandy Nash—Kentucky Gateway Museum

Eileen Yanoviak, executive director—Carnegie Center for Art and History

Orloff and Elisabeth Miller, archaeologists and historians, Mason/Bracken County

Regina Lang, local historian and researcher, Mason/Bracken County

Chanace Robert—Old Clock Church, New Albany

Carolyn Miller, historian and author, Mason/Bracken County

Martha Bladen, executive director—Switzerland County Historical Society

Chuck Parrish, retired historian—U.S. Army Corps of Engineers

Robert Bell, historian, member of the Twelfth U.S. Colored Calvary

Kathy Nichols, executive director—Farmington

Carol Ely, executive director—Locust Grove

Brian Cushing, program director—Locust Grove

Marion Lucas, PhD, historian and author, emeritus Professor—Western Kentucky University

Ashley Jordan, PhD—Evansville African American Museum

Diane Coon, historian and researcher

Thanks for the assistance from the Louisville Free Public Library, Cincinnati Public Library, Archives and Collections at the University of Louisville, Filson Historical Society and Kentucky Historical Society.

The National Park Service National Underground Railroad Network has been very valuable in documenting and working on this important time of United States history. I am grateful for their dedication and work.

Very special thanks to David Shuey and Gabriela Waesch, Ohio-Kentucky-Indiana Regional Council of Governments.

INTRODUCTION

The State of Ohio is separated from Kentucky just by one river; on either side of it the soil is equally fertile, and the situation equally favorable, and yet everything is different.

Here [in Ohio] *a population devoured by feverish activity, trying every means to make its fortune; the population seems poor to look at, for they work with their hands, but that work is the source of riches. There* [in Kentucky] *is a people which makes others work for it and shows little compassion, a people without energy, mettle or the spirit of enterprise...*

The population of Kentucky, which has been peopled for nearly a century, grows slowly. Ohio only joined the Confederation thirty years ago and has a million inhabitants. Within those thirty years Ohio has become the entrepot for the wealth that goes up and down the Mississippi; it has opened two canals and joined the Gulf of Mexico to the North Coast; meanwhile Kentucky, older and perhaps better placed, stood still.

These differences cannot be attributed to any other cause but slavery. It degrades the black population and enervates the white. Its fatal effects are recognized, and yet it is preserved and will be preserved for a long time more...
—Alexis de Toqueville, Democracy in America, *1835*

At the confluence of the Allegheny and Monongahela Rivers, the mighty Ohio River begins its 981-mile journey. It courses along six states with 664 of those miles running along Kentucky's border. As explorers and pioneers began to use the river in the late 1700s and early 1800s, the river had a 429-foot slope from its head at Pittsburgh to its

The Toqueville plaque commemorates Toqueville's stop at Westport on December 5, 1831, because the Ohio River was frozen. *Author's collection.*

mouth at the Mississippi River, creating shallow and hazardous riffles and chutes (such as the Falls of the Ohio in Louisville) to slow-moving pools and wide channels. The river had snags, rocks and drifting sandbars with a channel that constantly shifted. In those early years, the Ohio River was half of the size it is today. (Increased locks and management by the Army Corps of Engineers have widened and deepened the channels for commercial traffic.) Fluctuations between low- and high-water stages ranged from as little as a foot during severe droughts to as much as 80 feet during floods.[1] In spite of these hazards, it was the artery to the heart of a frontier with an abundance of natural resources to be exploited. With the Louisiana Purchase, the United States possessed the New Orleans port. By 1810–11, about 1,200 flatboats departed from the upper Ohio River or New Orleans, carrying 130,000 barrels of flour; 600,000 pounds of bacon; 10,000 barrels of whiskey; and huge quantities of butter, hemp, cheese, livestock and other commodities.[2]

Zodak Kramer was an eyewitness to the influx of immigrants who gathered in Pittsburgh to begin the journey down the Ohio. He captured the excitement and promise of the new frontier in his book *The Navigator* (1801):

Exclusive of the trading boats, there are many loaded altogether with merchandise of foreign importation, destined to Kentucky, Tennessee, Ohio and the territories. Many others are family boats, seeking places of settlement in these new countries, where their posterity may rest in safety, having plenty of all the necessaries, and any of the luxuries of life, where their children's children may enjoy the rich and prolifick [sic] productions of the land, without an over degree of toil or labour, where the climate is mild and the air are salubrious, where each man is a prince in his own kingdom and may without molestation, enjoy the frugal fare of his humble cot; where the clashing and terrifick [sic] sounds of war are not heard; where tyrants that desolate the earth dwell not; where man, simple man, is left to the guidance of his own will, subject only to laws of his own making, fraught with mildness, operating equally just on all, and by all protected and willingly obeyed.

The promise of this vision captures the American dream but falls short for the population of people who came to America as slaves. Enslavement was well engrained in society before the Revolutionary War. Enslaved people were part of the beginning of migrants who came to America and are documented as early as the 1500s with Spanish expeditions. Portuguese, Spanish, English, French, Dutch and others "collectively facilitated racial slavery" and "worked together" to facilitate the dislocation of indigenous people of Africa and the Americas.[3]

Indentures were another type of warrant that bound one person to another as America developed. The difference between enslaved and indentured servants is that indentures were a short-term agreement between the servant and master that guaranteed freedom after a period of service. Enslaved laborers were taken against their will. They were regarded as property to be traded, sold and forced to act under their slaveholder's desires. Even the tax laws regarded slaves as property, much like owning livestock. Slaveholders were taxed each year according to the number of slaves they owned. By going back through property tax records today, historians can identify slaveholders, which gives all kinds of context for community history and research.

Slavery was a life sentence. It was passed to the next generation on the maternal side—if your mother was enslaved, you were enslaved. This was part of culture from England, known as *partus sequitur ventrem*, in which the social status of a child comes from the mother. This eliminated the financial responsibilities of the father for children born into slavery. Thus, any child born to an enslaved woman was born into slavery, regardless of the citizenship or ancestry of the father. Manumission was the act of an owner setting his or her slaves free.

As the Constitution of the United States was being framed, southern delegates refused ratification unless specific provisions recognized and protected slavery. Slavery had become an established labor system for production of commodities such as rice, cotton, tobacco, corn and whiskey. There was continued support for the abolition of slavery, though, and the passing of the Slave Trade Act of 1807 was intended to close the slave trade by banning the importation of slaves into the United States. This simply fueled internal slave markets that encouraged slave trading within the states and resulted in slave trading, "breeding farms" and auction houses.

The rise of the internal slave trade in the United States corresponded to the increased demand for cotton from Great Britain. By 1860, Great Britain had become the center of the Industrial Revolution, and a large part of that industry was cotton textiles. The major supply of cotton (75 percent) for Britain's textile mills came from the southern United States. Cotton was vital to the economy of the United States, and the labor force came from enslaved laborers.[4] As slave numbers increased from the demand of labor in cotton and sugar cane fields, organized UGRR stations increased across the Ohio River—from Kentucky into Indiana and Ohio. This continued through the Civil War.

Kentucky was not a cotton state, nor did it support a large sugar cane industry. But what it could supply was the labor force needed in the South, as well as the production of crops like corn, tobacco and hemp (which was used to produce cotton bale and bags) and commodities like pork, whiskey, and wine. As the demand for field hands grew, states like Kentucky provided the necessary labor. Slave auction sites became common, and slave traders began to buy and hold slaves to ship them in larger groups to auction houses in Natchez and New Orleans.

Lexington held the largest public slave auctions in Kentucky at Cheapside (now a designated park between Upper and Mill Streets), close to the courthouse, sometimes drawing several thousand people.[5] Lexington's location in the center of the state made it more difficult for slaves to escape, and it had earned a reputation for selling "fancy girls," young women of mixed race sold for sex. Abraham Lincoln's wife, Mary Todd, came from a slaveholding family. Lincoln was visiting his wife's family in 1846 at the time that Mary's father, Richard Todd, purchased five slaves at Cheapside, and it is thought that Lincoln may have been present at the auction site.[6]

Louisville's location on the Ohio River made it an ideal place for slave traders to gather slaves for easy shipment to southern slave markets. The blocks between Jefferson and Main Streets, from First to Sixth, were where slave traders and slave auctioneers gathered, bought and sold enslaved humans like livestock. Individual slave sales were advertised with meeting places such as St. Charles Restaurant, the Louisville Hotel or even a street corner with a designated time and date. Slave traffickers boldly placed want ads in Louisville newspapers, such as the *Daily Democrat* and *Louisville Daily Courier*. The following are some of the Louisville slave traders who were listed in want ads: Mathew Garrison, D.S. Benedict and Son, J.W. Craig, M.V. Watts, Nathaniel Gaither, Hite and Tydings, W.P. Davis, E.V. Bunn, Jonathon B. McIlvain, Tarlton and Jonathan Arterburne, John Clark, M.V. Watts, James W. Brannon, Mathis and Duncan and W.M. Duncan.

By 1850, two major population centers had developed along Kentucky's borderline at the Ohio River: Cincinnati in free territory and Louisville in slave territory. Louisville was unique as the only major city in a largely rural state and as the only major city between Baltimore and St. Louis on the "slave side." African Americans accounted for 23.3 percent of Louisville's population in 1830. This was 2,406 people, of whom 300 were "free people of color." The number of African Americans in Louisville increased to 5,432 by 1850. Likewise, in Cincinnati, on the "free side" of the Ohio River, African Americans increased from 1,090 to 3,237 during the same time frame.[7]

The proximity of these two municipalities and the increasing steamboat trade along the Ohio River leading up to and through the Civil War became the battlefront on the question of slavery. As more and more people traveled along the river, the increasing visibility of shackled families became a haunting and disturbing image.

There was a sense by some slaveholders that the institution of slavery would become a distant memory as the United States continued to grow. Henry Clay of Kentucky chaired the American Colonization Society in 1817 by charter in Washington, D.C. Members established a colony on the West Coast of Africa, which became the nation of Liberia in 1847. The idea was to emigrate blacks back to Africa because it was believed and widely promoted that they would never assimilate into American culture. This was a time when uprisings such as John Brown at Harper's Ferry and Nat Turner's Rebellion were becoming more prevalent, causing some trepidation and concern among slaveholders that their own slaves may rebel against them.[8] In order to qualify to be sent to Liberia, slaveholders provided manumission papers if the enslaved agreed to go. The freed designees would be assigned a new name and were shipped to the new colony. By the Civil War, thirteen thousand colonists resided in Liberia, but it is thought that many thousands died from disease and sickness on their journey from the United States.[9]

The Ohio River was the defining place where visibility of trafficking eclipsed any notion of slavery as acceptable. As enslaved people began racing toward free soil, people in the North were no longer sanitized from the brutal realities of family separation, torture and death that resulted from slavery. Slavery was transparent.

This visibility was supported with the rise of American literature that favored abolition. Small printing presses became affordable, allowing for an explosion of newsprint, such as James Birney's the *Philanthropist*, Elijah Parish Lovejoy's *Alton Observer*, Cassius Clay's *True American*, William Lloyd Garrison's the *Liberator*, Henry Bibb's *Voice of the Fugitive* and Frederick Douglass's the *North Star*. The editors of these papers were threatened, beaten and their property was often destroyed. James Birney's press in New Richmond, Ohio, and Cassius Clay's printing press office in Lexington, Kentucky, were vandalized and burned; Frederick Douglass was beaten unconsciousness by a mob in Indiana; William Lloyd Garrison was dragged through the streets by a mob in Boston; Henry Bibb's press was burned in Canada; and Elijah Lovejoy's press was burned, and he was shot to death by a mob in Illinois. (Note: many of these newspapers have been digitized and are online—a simple Google search will take you to these online sites.)

Slaves who experienced the horrors "were claiming their voice" with more than one hundred narratives published between 1760 and 1860.[10] Examples include Henry Bibb's *The Life and Adventures of Henry Bibb: An American Slave* (1849); Frederick Douglass's *Narrative of the Life of Frederick Douglass, an American Slave* (1845); Josiah Henson's *The Life of Josiah Henson, Formerly a Slave* (1849); and Sojourner Truth's *Narrative of Sojourner Truth, a Northern Slave* (1850).

Abolitionist novels had a tremendous impact as a political tool to influence public opinion. The most well-known was Harriet Beecher Stowe's *Uncle Tom's Cabin* (1852), whose fictitious characters were based on real experiences from people mainly along the Ohio River border between Cincinnati and northern Kentucky, reaching to Ripley, Ohio, and Mason County, Kentucky. Mainstream American writers such as Henry Wadsworth Longfellow, John Greenleaf Whittier and Henry David Thoreau spoke out against slavery both publicly and in their work. Politicians such as Samuel Chase (Cincinnati attorney, U.S. Supreme Court justice under Abraham Lincoln), Cassius Clay (Kentucky politician and Russian ambassador), Ulysses Grant (Union general and U.S. president) and Richard James Oglesby (Oldham County, Kentucky, native, Union general and three times governor of Illinois) were important advocates for the abolition of slavery.

Another important contribution were the academies and seminaries that formed to support antislavery causes. The most well-known is Oberlin College in northern Ohio, which helped train students as UGRR conductors and then planted them, under disguise, in slave states. Delia Webster, who conducted in Lexington and Trimble County, is an example of such as student from Oberlin. Lane Seminary and the Farmer's College in Cincinnati, Ohio; Eleutherian College in Madison, Indiana; Augusta College in Augusta, Kentucky; and Berea College in Berea, Kentucky, were active in the debates on slavery. Eleutherian, Berea and Lane opened their doors to black students.

The free black communities on both sides of the river worked together to harbor and assist freedom seekers. W.H. Gibson Sr. wrote his narrative, *Fifty Years' Experience and a Participant in the Joys and Sorrows of His People from the Year 1847–1897*, about living in Louisville as a free black. Gibson, along with other free blacks in Louisville, such as Washington Spradling, Byrd Parker, William H. Miles and Jesse Meriwether, organized churches, schools, choirs, businesses and associations that also allowed the attendance of slaves (with permission of the slaveholder).

Organizations emerged that raised funds to support antislavery causes. The two most notable organized associations were the Anti-Slavery Society and the American Missionary Society. The Anti-Slavery Society, organized by William Lloyd Garrison in 1833, became the arm of the abolitionist movement with auxiliary antislavery societies quickly lining themselves along the borderland of the Ohio River. The groups gave voice to citizens who opposed slavery, empowering people to organize and assist refugee slaves and influence politics at the grassroots level.

The American Missionary Association (AMA) was organized on Christian principles in 1846 to abolish slavery and educate African Americans. Founded by a board of both blacks and whites, the association played a tremendous role in establishing schools and colleges for blacks, including Howard University, Berea College, Talladega College and Fisk University, among others. John Fee from Kentucky worked with Cassius Clay to establish Berea College with the support of the AMA. The association largely comprised Congressionalist Church members.

The American Bible Society (ABS), organized in 1816, was founded by people who committed to spreading the word of the Bible and ending slavery.

The ABS identified leaders in communities to help distribute Bibles, which included placing Bibles in the hands of slaves. The distribution of Bibles took on a more radical effort where colporteurs were hired to personally deliver Bibles to slaves in the field and served as points of contact for enslaved laborers who wanted to escape.

Colporteurs were recognized by most communities as traveling salesman and were accepted because their mission was viewed as an asset to convert slaves to Christianity. Their hidden agenda, however, was to encourage slaves to run, and they provided information on how to travel through the UGRR to Canada. The ABS often partnered with the AMA, and colporteurs were financed through these associations.

White churches often allowed slaves to be baptized and become members of the church. This gesture demonstrated redemption and benevolence from the slaveholder's perspective. As more blacks became members, black churches sprang up with support from parent churches. The Methodist Church did not support slavery, but to establish itself in slave states, it accommodated slavery as part of the legal system. In Louisville alone there were at least eight black churches in operation before the Civil War, and four of them became known centers for UGRR activities. These churches became places to meet, organize and support one another, as well as antislavery causes.[11]

Methodism was the most popular religion among blacks in Kentucky. The Methodist Episcopal Church's 1845 conference in Kentucky listed 39,756 white and 9,362 black participants. In 1846, the conference spilt into two sessions: the Louisville conference and the Kentucky conference, with total members rising to 54,411.[12]

Conventions and conferences were organized in Detroit, New York and Boston that gathered to raise funds and bring attention to the plight of enslaved people. Sojourner Truth, Frederick Douglass, Harriet Tubman, Henry Bibb, Josiah Henson and Lewis Hayden gave testimony in courts, conferences, churches and public forums to share their firsthand experiences of slavery. The Michigan State Anti-Slavery Society, American Anti-Slavery Society, Michigan Convention of Colored Citizens and American Missionary Society are just a small number of organizations that quickly organized and grew with associations of smaller groups. In addition, vigilance committees were formed in small and large communities, particularly along the river. These committees provided assistance for fugitives and those discriminated against.

Greed made it difficult for slave owners who did not want to give up their investments made on human property. A person was an investment for the slaveholder. An investment worth $1,200 (in human chattel) one day would be of no monetary value the next day if slavery was to end. To calculate equivalency of dollars in today's market for an enslaved person in the 1850s, use the following: Take the average amount given for a slave (usually $700) and divide it by 7.6 (today's inflation rate) then multiply that by 100. For example, from the Oldham County Historical Society Records: $700 \div 7.6 = 92.105$, then $92.105 \times 100 = 9,210.52$. So, $9,210.52 would be the modern-day price of a slave that would have sold for $700 in the 1850s.

The system of slaveholding was profitable to those who held slaves, as well as the auction houses, bounty hunters, jailors and other public officials. Court-appointed officials, such as justices of the peace and locally appointed jailors and sheriffs, were given money for bringing in runaways. Not only did the court offer rewards for runaway slaves, but slaveholders would also pay additional money to slave catchers, who sometimes included public officials. Jails used slave labor in rock quarries, hemp production and other intensive, physical tasks, making money that went into pockets of officials as well as supporting local pursuits. Slaveholders paid taxes on their slaves, just like other property, each year. These taxes went into the county resources to support county projects.

Slaveholders could also hire out their human property. If a local farmer or business needed help, that farmer or business could temporarily hire the enslaved laborer from the slaveholder. This became beneficial to the slaveholder when there wasn't enough work for their slaves during various seasons throughout the year. The slaveholder could earn additional income. The hire-out agreement included the responsibility of the slave's upkeep (food, clothing and board). Oldham County Court documents show cases of lawsuits where the renter (defendant) did not pay or refused to return the slave to the owner (plaintiff). There are also suits where the plaintiff accused the defendant of improper treatment of the slave. Lastly, some slaveholders would allow the enslaved to seek employment when available to earn payment for emancipation.

In counties that bordered the Ohio River, slaveholders hired out their slaves to industries across the river, including ship builders. The laborers would ferry across during the day and return to their slaveholder at night. Of course, the opportunity for escape often presented itself, which was what happened in the case of Henry Bibb, when his slaveholder, William Gatewood, gave him permission to work in the pork house in Madison, and Bibb escaped on a boat to Cincinnati.[13]

Example of a slave hire-out document. *Oldham County Historical Society*.

As the Civil War approached, the institution of slavery was falling apart at the seams. In 1833, Great Britain passed the Slave Emancipation Act, which gave all slaves in the British Empire their freedom, though there were stipulations. The act became law on August 1, 1834, and had rippling effects across the ocean, particularly in the United States, where it was celebrated as Liberation Day in free states.

By the 1840s, the mercantile trade in Great Britain had started to shift to the purchase of raw materials from their colonies, which decreased the demand of tobacco, sugar cane and cotton from the United States. The railroad was replacing the steamboat and could reach farther inland, diversifying markets for the individual farmer who could transport livestock, produce and commodities more efficiently and effectively and at a cheaper price. The railways were expanding westward, opening the new frontier for exploration and exploitation. The notion of individualism and personal freedom made slavery less palatable for an expanding democracy.

ESCAPE ROUTES

Railroads

By 1850, the use of trains was integrated into the UGRR. This corresponded with the completion of rail lines northward into Canada. Fugitives were concealed in freight cars, and in some cases, vigilance groups purchased tickets for these secreted passengers in disguise. The railroad tracks provided a path to follow as they guided travelers north. Some railroads were known for their active "secreting of fugitives."[14] Conductor I. Newton Pierce in Alliance, Ohio, had an understanding with all the passenger train conductors on the Connecticut and Western Railroad "that colored persons with tickets bearing 'I.N.P.'" were to be admitted to trains "without question, unless slave-catchers were thought to be aboard."[15] The Northern Central Railroad was used by UGRR conductors Jervis Langdon and John Jones, who placed fugitives in the baggage car at four o'clock in the morning at Elmira, New York, and traveled directly, without charge, to the Niagara River. Fugitives were known to take the Mad River Railroad, which traveled from Urbana through Cincinnati and Dayton to the destination at Lake Erie.

When railroads began to appear on the American landscape, they were often privately owned and had short lines with lack of continuity that made direct connections between larger cities. Passengers often had to connect several times to complete their routes. This was the case for New Albany native and UGRR conductor Henson McIntosh, who helped fugitives Frank and Betty escape from Louisville. Ferrying with the fugitives from Portland, across the Ohio River and into New Albany, they caught the New Albany and Salem train to Mitchell and then transferred to the Ohio and Mississippi Railroad through Madison and Cincinnati. They were caught and apprehended by Louisville police on the eastbound train. McIntosh spent several years in the Kentucky penitentiary.[16]

Canals

In 1825, Ohio passed legislation to begin construction of two canals: the Miami and Erie Canal from Cincinnati to Toledo, connecting the Ohio River to Lake Erie and the Ohio and Erie Canal, which connected Cleveland to Portsmouth. The Miami and Erie Canal was completed in 1845. The vision was to connect the Ohio River to the Great Lakes and

Visitors can ride on a canal boat and experience this restored section of the Whitewater Canal Historic District in Metamora, Indiana. *Author's collection.*

open access for more market goods to be shipped from the South to the North. The canals were built twenty-six feet wide at the bottom and forty feet wide at the water surface. The water was four feet deep, and the tow path was ten feet wide. Tow paths along the canals were cleared so boats could be pulled, usually by mules, along the man-made waterway. The canals were completed as the railroads were built. The slowness of the boats could not compete with railroad transportation for passengers and perishable goods, but they could carry large cargo, such as grains and salted pork. During the winter months, the canals were frozen, which made them inoperable.

In Indiana, the Wabash and Erie Canal began operation in 1843. It was 497 miles long, reaching from Toledo, Ohio, to Evansville, Indiana, on the Ohio River, making it the longest canal in North America. The Wabash and Erie Canal was a well-known thoroughfare for slaves, who followed it from the vicinity of Evansville until they reached Ohio, traveling as far as Toledo.[17] Once in Cleveland and other canal cities bordering the Great Lakes, a boat could be taken to Canada. Much like the Miami and Erie Canal that began in Cincinnati, the canals were hard to maintain and could not compete with railroads.

There were many mills erected along the banks of the canals, which were constructed for both navigation and hydraulic power. These mills were erected to manufacture flour and woolen products. On the section of canal built into Cincinnati, water was used to power some ninety runs of stones. A pair of burr stones was considered a run, so there were many mills along this section. In many instances, as the canals became obsolete for towing, railroads acquired rights to build on the old tow paths. The established canal tow paths provided easy access for fugitives who could cross the borderland of the Ohio River and follow the canals, as witnessed by a canal worker in Siebert's book:

> *We used to see, occasionally, the fugitives, who ventured out for exercise while waiting for an opportunity to get on one of the vessels frequently passing down the canal and river from Milan, during the season of navigation. Many of these vessels passed through the Welland Canal on their way to the lower Lakes, and after leaving the harbor at Huron the fugitives were safe from the pursuit of their masters unless the vessels were compelled by stress of weather to return to the harbor.*[18]

Steamboats

When the first steamboat, the *New Orleans*, made its way down the Ohio River, its hull was too deep to carry cargo and passengers, but it was a symbol of the future that changed the Ohio River forever. No longer was the river a one-way passage. Now boats could travel up and down stream, increasing commerce and travel. Steamboats were modified with shallow hulls that made them more accessible to land along shores, and soon, small river towns began to thrive. In addition, Portland Canal in Louisville was built in 1825 to bypass the Falls of the Ohio, which had been the only navigational barrier on the river. Prior to its construction, boats were portaged through, which made for a slower and more arduous passing.

Pittsburgh, Cincinnati, Vevay, Jeffersonville and Evansville are just a few of the towns that became important shipyards for steamboat construction. Slave labor was involved in every aspect of the shipping industry, including foundries, fuels, portage, transport, ship maintenance, food preparation in the galleys and cleaning chambers on ships. Even music was provided by enslaved labor. Many slaves crossed the river to free soil shipping ports and returned across the river to home at the end of the day. Some slaves

Louisville waterfront in the late nineteenth century. *P0228, Archives and Special Collections, University of Louisville.*

traveled with the ships from port to port on extended leaves from their homes and slaveholders. According to the 1845 Louisville Directory, the amount of traffic in 1845, on the Ohio River documents thousands of tons of commerce; 1,476 steamboats and 168 flat and packet boats went through the Louisville and Portland Canal Company. At the Portland Canal in Louisville, $1,368,015.17 was collected in tolls during 1845. In today's equivalency that would amount to $18,000,592.

Counties located along the river had many landings along their shores. Flatboats, steamboats and packets could line up along these landings, giving easy trade access. Almost every farm located along the river had a landing or shared one with a neighbor. According to steamboat history expert Travis C. Vasconcelos, these landings not only shipped their commodities but also provided needed timber to fuel the various boats. The boats were often in competition with each other to pick up commodities so they could profit in procuring and trading at shipping ports. In the height of the steamboat era leading up to the Civil War, even small farms needed extra hands to supply the commodities. At this time, most boats were fueled by wood, so large amounts of cut timber were needed. This provided additional profit opportunities for farmers at these landings.

The following list of landings covers a twenty-eight-mile section of the river between Louisville and Milton, Kentucky (Milton is located across from Madison, Indiana):

River Ports and Landings between Louisville and Milton, KY
Log Book of Boaz & Corka, 1906–1918 (28 miles):

Kentucky Side: Harrods Creek, Miller's Foot, Duersons (2 landings) Barbour's Ditch, Harmony Landing, Woolfork's Landing, Taylors Creek, Bottorff's Landing, Tarleton's Landing, Schroters Ditch, Reed's Landing, Hall's Landing, Mead's Landing, Upper & Lower, Jacob's 2 Landings, Eighteen Mile Light, Westport, Houston's Light, Walter Luckett's Landing, Oldham Landing, Pattons Creek, Abbott's Landing, Wise's Landing, Corn Creek Spring Creek, Adam's Landing, Pandeller's Landing, Page's Landing, Hites Landing, Milton
Indiana Side: Howards Shipyard Landing, Ash Brother Six Mile Landing, Wover's Landing, Charley Goddwin's Landing, Utica, Lents Limekill, Amos Goodwin's Landing, Kemp's Light Landing, Robinson's Landing, Hopkin's Landing, Immigration Landing, Fern Grove, Rodman's Light Landing, Haymaker Light Landing, Round's Landing, Big Gut Landing, Bull Creek Landing.[19]

It will be never be known how many fugitives actually used steamboats for escape, but the borderland of the Ohio River and its promise of free soil made the boats a viable risk worth taking. Ads like the following were fairly common in local newspapers:

Runaway
On Sunday, the 11th INSTANT. FROM the steamer Peytona, a negro man named BEN, the slave of Collin Throckmorton, of Daviess county, Ky. Said Slave was hired on said boat, and a liberal reward will be paid for his return to the undersigned at Louisville, Ky.
D.S. Benedict & Son.

In the thirty-first congress, Senator Jefferson Davis of Mississippi commented, "Negros do escape from Mississippi frequently and the boats constantly passing by our long line of river frontier furnish great facility to get into Ohio; and when they do escape it is with great difficulty that they are recovered, indeed, it seldom occurs that they are restored."[20]

This book highlights the UGRR that operated along the border of the Ohio River for several reasons. One is that the cases are well defined, so the tour can take visitors to places and sites that have been well documented. The proximity of the free soil and slave soil along the Ohio River give a visibility of separation, which cannot be experienced in any other setting. The Ohio River demonstrates that the flow of escape was often west to east, as well as south to north. And boat captains ferried many fugitives to free soil.[21] The Ohio River was an open corridor of escape, providing the abundance of river traffic as concealment for those taking the risk of running.

HOW TO USE THIS BOOK

The tour goes from west to east along the Ohio River. Each of the five chapters can be toured separately. Obviously, the larger metropolitan areas, such as Louisville and Cincinnati, provide more museums and house tours than smaller communities. However, the smaller towns and rural areas provide a perspective of the distance and difficulty that freedom seekers faced, and the risk for conductors was greater because smaller communities were more connected and people knew each other. The vistas and charm of the small river towns offer an opportunity of peaceful reflection and beauty. The Ohio River remains an awesome ecological wonder even though it is continually threatened by development and industry.

The places that are suggested to visit at the end of the chapter do not always connect to the history of the UGRR; however, they often give a natural history and geographic perspective of the way people traveled and communicated during antebellum America. The following gives a brief summary of the tours.

Chapter 1: "The Western Reaches of the Ohio River" includes Owensboro and Brandenburg, Kentucky, and Evansville and Corydon, Indiana. Evansville became a significant steamboat port, and its canal provided direct northern access for freedom seekers. Owensboro was home to Josiah Henson, who was the model for Uncle Tom in Harriet Beecher Stowe's novel.

Chapter 2: "Louisville's Slave Trade" includes Louisville, Kentucky, and New Albany and Jeffersonville, Indiana. Louisville was the largest metropolitan area for slave trading along the Ohio River. As a result, New Albany became a channel for fugitives who often came through the Portland area of Louisville.

Chapter 3: "The Shallows to Madison" includes the area of the Ohio River around Madison, Indiana, where the water was sometimes as low as four feet, which allowed for easy crossing of the river. This section was also narrow and would often freeze over. This area includes Madison and Vevay, Indiana, and Oldham, Trimble County and Carroll County, Kentucky. There were some very high-profile conductors such as Delia Webster, George DeBaptiste, Elijah Anderson and Chapman Harris around the Madison area with a few free black settlements. Madison was the first escape site for Henry Bibb, who jumped on a steamboat to Cincinnati.

Chapter 4: "A Free Metropolis" is the region around Cincinnati. As a free side of the river, Cincinnati was the most logical site for the UGRR because of its thriving metropolis. Historian, author and UGRR researcher Wilbur Siebert thought there were more escapes here than any other place along the river. The area includes Rising Sun, Aurora and Lawrenceburg, Indiana, and Cincinnati and New Richmond (Clermont County Freedom Trail), Ohio, and Boone County, Covington and Newport, Kentucky.

Chapter 5: "A Community Connected" focuses on the Ripley, Ohio region. A small town, Ripley was home to some very active UGRR conductors who organized to take fugitives north. Its proximity to Maysville and the Paris Pike in Kentucky gave it a significant advantage. Paris Pike was the main frontier road from the Ohio River leading to the interior bluegrass region surrounding Lexington, which was a large slave trading center. This region encompasses Point Pleasant and Ripley, Ohio, and Maysville, Augusta, Washington and Germantown, Kentucky.

The tour travels, for the most part, along Scenic Byways that have been established on both sides of the Ohio River. The span and beauty of the Ohio River can be viewed on both sides with vistas high on the ridge, such as the John Rankin House in Ripley or shoreside routes with walkways, parks and bicycle paths (including a daily ferry crossing the Ohio River in Augusta, Kentucky) that have been established through municipalities and county parks. The route ventures into small towns and large cities (Louisville and Cincinnati), all of which have created historic districts and preservation programs to capture the context of life along the river in years past.

Most communities that are highlighted have museums where you can learn more about the community and the UGRR. There are historical markers placed at various sites recognizing slavery, slave escapes and noted abolitionists, and many of these places are documented as members of the National Park Service National Underground Railroad Network.

This book could not possibly recognize all the attempts of escape along this route. I emphasized the most notable of record with researched associations. This book will highlight some of the conductors and fugitives, including Washington Spradley, Bird Parker, W.H. Gibson, Calvin Fairbank, Levi and Catherine Coffin, Henry Bibb, George DeBaptiste, Elijah Anderson, Laura Haviland, Harriet Beecher Stowe, Delia Webster, John Van Zandt, Josiah Henson, Juliet Miles, John Rankin and his family, John and Matilda Fee, Thorton Blackburn, Eliza Harris, James Birney, John and Matilda Fee, Salmon Chase, John Parker and his family, Margaret Garner and Cassius Clay, among others. Most of these people have biographies, autobiographies and narratives that can be further investigated by a simple Google search of their names.

Resistance to slavery was common and dealt with severely by slaveholders. Whippings, brandings, and shackles, as well as torture and even death were used to deter slaves from escaping. Only first names were used to distinguish individuals, making sure the surnames were omitted so families could not connect. There are numerous stories in which enslaved people resisted the attempt to flee because they would be separated from their loved ones.

Historic court records show many accounts of resistance in which people sacrificed themselves for justice. The first murder on record in Oldham County was "Lucy, Woman of Color, ground glass in a stew and gave it to Elizabeth Smith, her slaveholder"[22] The number of freedom seekers who attempted and were successful at their escape will never be known. The National Park Service estimates that there were thousands of escapes that had no assistance through the UGRR. The Underground Railroad became more organized as the increasing numbers of slaves in the South corresponded to the rise of the cotton and sugar cane production during the 1830s, leading to the Civil War. Black leadership took hold as an increasing number of fugitives told their stories and went back across the border to rescue more family and friends. Free black communities within slaveholding states organized through churches and masonic organizations to provide assistance. Others began to work with blacks to organize and help through antislavery societies, academies, missionaries and the free press.

The organization of the UGRR is a chapter in United States history that demonstrates the incredible courage of people who worked together to make the world better for everyone. The cast of evil over good is played out in the human theater. The stories of the past are more captivating when

Credits: The Oldham County Historical Society, National Park Service National Underground Railroad Network Site Airbus,USGS,NGA,NASA,CGIAR,NCEAS,NLS,OS,NMA,Geodatastyrelsen,GSA,GSI and the GIS User Community

This map shows Underground Railroad sites highlighted in this book. *Cartography by OKI, 2019. The Oldham County Historical Society, National Park Service National Underground Railroad Network Site Airbus, USGS, NGA, NASA, CGIAR, NCEAS, NLS, OS, NMA, Geodatastyrelsen, GSA, GSI and the GIS User Community.*

told through local communities in the place where they occurred. These places hold the power and magic of human spirit that can be experienced in context of where lives were lived, where courage was tested and where sacrifices were made.

THE WESTERN REACHES OF THE OHIO RIVER

*Evansville and Corydon, Indiana,
and Owensboro and Brandenburg, Kentucky*

When the Northwest Ordinance was passed in 1787, the Ohio River became the geographic division between slave states and free states. Kentucky achieved statehood in 1792, but the states formed from the Northwest Territory, Ohio (1803), Indiana (1816), Illinois (1818), Michigan (1837), Wisconsin (1848) and Minnesota (1858), were yet to be defined. Even though these areas were declared free states, slavery continued in various forms with restrictions known as Black Codes. Slaveholders who moved into these areas made their slaves sign indenture agreements. Illinois included clauses within its Black Codes that stated that recaptured escaped slaves would have time added to their indentures.

With the rise of the steamboat era, trade and businesses became more aggressive along the shores of the Ohio River, and the need for laborers created a blurred mix of free workers and enslaved laborers. Opportunities for fugitives along the southwestern reaches of the Kentucky border were more difficult because of the proximity to more slave states. At the southwest edges of the Ohio River slavecatchers from Missouri would kidnap free blacks or recapture escaped slaves. Free blacks were then taken to Missouri and sold where it was legal. The U.S. government exploited the slave labor in this section as well by hiring out more than one thousand slaves to run its saltworks operation near Shawneetown, Illinois (supposedly free soil). The salt was important during these years for preservation of food.[23]

As the larger city in the region on the free side of the river, Evansville introduced Abraham Lincoln (1809–1865) to the complexities of life in a

ROUTES THROUGH INDIANA AND MICHIGAN
IN 1848.

As traced by Lewis Falley.

Underground Railroad Routes traced by Lewis Falley in 1848. *From Wilbur H. Siebert, The Underground Railroad from Slavery to Freedom.*

privileged democracy where distinctions were made between race and gender. Born in Kentucky, Lincoln moved with his family to southern Indiana in 1816. He lived thirty-five miles from the Ohio River, northeast of Evansville, Indiana, from ages seven to twenty-one. Lincoln's parents, Thomas and Nancy, were antislavery and were caught in land disputes in Kentucky, so the move to the new state of Indiana offered promise and opportunity.

Abe Lincoln became familiar with life on the Ohio River when he was hired by one of his father's friends to operate a ferry near Evansville. Lincoln would ferry passengers over the Anderson River where it flowed into the Ohio in a small rowboat. In the winter of 1828–29, Lincoln and Allen Gentry were hired by Allen's father to pilot a flatboat to New Orleans. They did so successfully, after much hardship, and returned by steamboat to Indiana. As they guided the flatboat, selling produce along the way, they would have experienced diverse populations and witnessed slavery at large scale on plantations in the South.[24] Evansville, by this time, was a successful river port.

Two major canals were constructed around this time on the Ohio River: the Miami and Erie Canal at Cincinnati that began construction in 1825 and the Wabash and Erie Canal at Evansville that began construction in 1832. Both of the canals proved to be disasters. The idea was to link the Ohio River to Lake Erie, giving shipping access from the heart of the United States to the gateway of the New Orleans ports. But the canals, which were shallow, froze during winter months, and the construction was delayed more than fifteen years, partly due to a national economic slump. As the canals were being constructed, the railroad was aggressively extended, making it difficult for canals, which used mules and manual labor to pull the canal boats, to compete with trains. What the canals did provide, however, was a way for fugitives to follow a northern path to freedom

By 1852, Evansville was connected by packet boat lines with places on the Green, Wabash, Cumberland, Tennessee and Ohio Rivers. This region between Kentucky and Indiana was fertile ground, high in corn production, tobacco and livestock. The low-lying land was rich in deep black river soil and contained deposits of coal that was more accessible than that mountain regions in the east. Just like the upper reaches of the Ohio River, packets would stop at private landings and carry freight, passengers and mail along the river routes. In 1865, 2,500 steamboats were docked at Evansville. As the largest regional river port downstream from Louisville, Evansville became an obvious escape route for fugitives to follow.

LIBERTY BAPTIST CHURCH, EVANSVILLE

Evansville had only a small population of free blacks prior to the Civil War, but it was enough to provide assistance on the UGRR. Today, the Liberty Baptist Church, organized on June 13, 1865, stands as a historical marker for the black community. The church was organized two months after the Civil War ended as a testament to the fact that blacks were eager to support the welfare of the migration of blacks who crossed the Ohio River. Blacks quickly moved to the area around the church, which became known as Baptist Town. The black population grew from ninety-five in 1860 to almost two thousand by 1870. The church, located at 701 Oak Street, began as a small, frame building and gave rise to a larger, Gothic structure built in 1886, which still stands today. The church has provided leadership and social structure for the black community, and other churches have developed from this parent congregation.

WILLARD CARPENTER: EVANSVILLE UNDERGROUND RAILROAD CONDUCTOR

Born on a farm in Vermont in 1803, Carpenter followed the course of his generation and headed westward to seek fortune and opportunity. He took many jobs, including that of a teacher—a common circumstance for young men—as he moved from place to place, eventually joining his brother in the mercantile trade. The Carpenter brothers did well for themselves, with a third brother joining the business that eventually settled in Evansville. Willard expanded his business to include a hotel and stables that could accommodate fifty horses. Soon, Carpenter got involved in politics and sponsored efforts for the Wabash Erie Canal and the Evansville and Crawfordsville Railroad.

Willard had great sympathy for charitable causes and established houses for the poor and a hospital. He was also opposed to slavery and became a conductor on the Underground Railroad. His home, completed in 1849 and still standing today, was a popular landmark for the young city. The house walls were twenty-one-inch-thick brick, and furniture was imported from New York and Europe. The stables that Carpenter owned were known to have hid many fugitive slaves on their first stop crossing the river.[25]

Other notable UGRR conductors in the Evansville and Vanderburg County area were Judge A.L. Robinson, who personally defended ten young fishermen prosecuted for ferrying fugitives across the Ohio and J.G. Jones, real estate man in Evansville, as well as Patrick and Robert Calvert, Joseph Carter and Robert Armstrong, Judge Gaines Roberts and Abraham Phelps, James Caswell, John Hill, Colonel J.W. Cockrum, Frank Posey, Reverend Hopkins and Conrad Baker.

THE JOSIAH HENSON STORY FROM OWENSBORO, KENTUCKY

Owensboro was on the "yellow banks" of the Ohio River, upstream from Evansville, Indiana. Situated in Daviess County, which was formed in 1815, the land was rich in minerals, with one of the earliest coal mines in the area, the Bon Harbor Coal Mine that ran a rail line to the Ohio River. The 1840 census records showed 6,327 whites, 44 free colored and 1,960 slaves populated the county. One of the most famous nineteenth-century Americans, Josiah Henson (1789–1882), was enslaved here for a number of years until his escape. His story became partially immortalized when Harriet Beecher Stowe used Henson's profile as her Uncle Tom in *Uncle Tom's Cabin*.

The Josiah Henson Trail is marked by a couple of signs leading east on US 60 from Owensboro. Following the trail for about fifteen miles northeast, a Kentucky historical marker designates the site where Josiah Henson fled from the Riley plantation with his wife and three children, making it safely to Canada in a long and arduous journey. Once in Canada, Henson published his narrative in 1849, *The Life of Josiah Henson, Formerly a Slave, Now an Inhabitant of Canada, as Narrated by Himself*, which became a popular story that circulated throughout the northern states.

Born into slavery, Henson's first childhood memory was of his father being whipped and tortured and then sold south, for defending his mother, who was being raped by a white man. Henson and his mother were traded to Isaac Riley, who lived near Washington, D.C. Henson became the overseer for Riley. Isaac was a gambler and acquired mounting debts, so he decided to send his slaves to his brother, Amos Riley, who lived outside of Owensboro, to keep from having his slaves seized for debts owed. Josiah was entrusted to take the enslaved laborers to Amos and did so in a boat down the Ohio River. The group included eighteen slaves and Henson's wife and children. At a stop in Cincinnati on free soil, where people tried to convince Henson and his entourage to escape and flee north, Henson resisted the temptation. Henson was intent on purchasing his freedom and was a man of honor who did not want to break his trust with Riley—a decision he later regretted. He delivered the slaves to Amos as promised.

Amos Riley had a large plantation, with close to one hundred slaves. During the next few years, Josiah and his family worked for Amos Riley, expecting Isaac to join his brother and move to Kentucky. Isaac decided to stay in Maryland, which caused Josiah to take a trip to visit and ask for the opportunity to purchase his freedom. A well-known white Methodist minister encouraged Josiah to earn money by preaching to help finance his manumission fee. The minister told Josiah to travel back to his master in Maryland, and on the journey, the minister would arrange for places where he could visit and speak, including an annual Methodist Conference at Chillicothe.

The journey to Maryland took Josiah three months. All the while he preached and visited congregations, earning money for his manumission. Once arriving in Maryland, the fee of $450 was set for Josiah to pay for his freedom papers. Josiah paid $350. Isaac sealed the manumission document to give to Amos. It explained the deal for Josiah to earn the additional $100. He allowed Josiah to carry the sealed document back to Daviess County to Amos. When Josiah got back to Kentucky, Amos asked for the manumission papers and told Josiah that Isaac indicated he had $1,000 left to raise. Josiah realized he had been tricked and told Amos he had lost his manumission sealed document. Another year passed as Josiah worked on the Amos Riley farm, knowing he could never raise the money, but he also kept his freedom papers hidden.

Isaac hired an agent to sell his slaves, except for Josiah and his family, in Kentucky. Isaac also realized that Josiah would never be able to raise the remaining dollars and would more than likely try to escape. Isaac told Amos to sell Josiah in New Orleans on the next cargo shipment downriver. Amos accompanied Josiah, and when they reached New Orleans, several planters came to look over Josiah for purchase. As fate would have it, Amos became deathly sick with only Josiah to attend him. Josiah purchased their steamboat tickets back to Kentucky while nursing Amos back to health. This trick of fate allowed Josiah to return to his family—this time with a plan of escape.

Josiah; his wife, Charlotte; and their three children successfully fled, rowing across the Ohio River and making a difficult, long journey to Canada. In Canada, Josiah became friends with other fugitives, such as Henry Bibb, and they worked together to set up supplies and opportunities for refugees. He established the Dawn Settlement School in Dresden, Canada, including the British American School, which focused on industrial training. He, like Henry Bibb, traveled frequently to the United States to raise funds. He also took a trip to Great Britain in 1851, where Henson was granted a personal audience with Queen Victoria. He also acted as a conductor on the Underground Railroad. He journeyed back into slave territory and helped more than two hundred freedom seekers. With the publication of his narrative and his outstanding skills as orator, he caught the attention of Harriet Beecher Stowe as she was penning her novel *Uncle Tom's Cabin*.

Henson met Stowe when she invited him and a friend to her home in Andover, Maryland, after reading his story. In her book *A Key to Uncle Tom's Cabin; the Original Facts and Documents Upon Which the Story is Founded* (1853), Stowe credits Josiah Henson as her parallel model for Uncle Tom in her book. In 1983, Josiah Henson became the first black person to be featured on a Canadian postage stamp.

SCENIC BYWAYS

Ohio Scenic Byway: The Ohio Scenic Byway begins in Cairo, Illinois, and follows the course of the Ohio River, passing through three states: Illinois, Indiana and Ohio. From Evansville follow Highway 66 to Corydon, then up the river. See interactive internet map: http://ohioriverbyway.com/maps.

PLACES TO VISIT

INDIANA SIDE

Evansville

Willard Carpenter House

Entrepreneur and businessman Willard Carpenter built this house in 1849, and it is known for its unusual Georgian architecture with twenty-one-inch-thick walls. Carpenter was a philanthropist and known sympathizer for antislavery causes. The area around the house also had several sites for the Underground Railroad. A stone tunnel led from the river, three blocks north, to the Carpenters' basement, where fugitives hid until they could be relayed farther north. Other hiding places included Carpenter's stables

Willard Carpenter House was a known **UGRR** stop in Evansville. *Author's collection.*

nearby, which no longer exist. The Willard Carpenter House is owned by a local broadcast company, WNIN. There is a historical marker, but the house itself is not open to the public.

Website: www.indianalandmarks.org
Address: 413 Carpenter Street, Evansville, Indiana

The Evansville African American Museum

The Evansville African American Museum is the former home of the 1938 Federal Housing Project Lincoln Gardens, which was a part of President Roosevelt's New Deal. Part of the museum is dedicated to this time in Evansville history, depicting life during the 1930s. Other exhibits focus on the civil rights movement and local notables. There is an admission charge.

Website: www.evvafricanamericanmuseum.org,
Address: 579 South Garvin Street, Evansville, Indiana
Phone: (812) 423-5188

Evansville African American Museum interprets local history and contributions of African Americans in Evansville. *Author's collection.*

Liberty Baptist Church

Liberty Baptist Church is the oldest extant black congregation in Evansville. This is a mother church of the area from which many others sprang. Still active today, it is the center of the original black neighborhood known as Baptist Town. The large Gothic building, built in 1886, began as a small cabin at the close of the Civil War. It was known for activity of free blacks who participated on the UGRR.

Address: 701 Oak Street, Evansville, Indiana

Evansville Museum of Arts, History and Science

The museum complex is located along the Evansville waterfront, with walkways and children's playgrounds close by. It has many hands-on activities, a theater and a large building dedicated to transportation, including the history of trains, steamboats, the canal and horse-drawn carriages, which would have been prevalent during the UGRR.

Website: www.evansvillemuseum.org
Address: 411 South East Riverside Drive, Evansville, Indiana
Phone: (812) 425-2406

Lincoln Boyhood Memorial, National Park Service Site

Located thirty-five miles north of Evansville, this is where Lincoln spent his life from the ages of seven to twenty-one. The site includes a re-created 1820s homestead on 4 of the original 160 acres owned by Thomas Lincoln, Abe's father. There are hiking trails, a pioneer cemetery where Nancy Lincoln is buried and memorial building with sculptured panels. There is an admission charge.

Website: www.nps.gov/libo/index.htm
Address: 3027 East South Street, Lincoln City, Indiana

Corydon

Corydon Capitol State Historic Site

This site commemorates Indiana's first state capitol and follows development of Indiana from a territory to a state. The town has preserved the capitol and surrounding historic buildings, such as the governor's headquarters and law office. It was the site of the first slavery case in Indiana, *State vs. Lasselle*, where Polly sued her slaveholder, General Hyacinth Lasselle, for her freedom. Lasselle had purchased Polly's mother from Native Americans before Indiana had become a state. Through appeal, Polly's case went to the Indiana Supreme Court, which ruled in Polly's favor. There are guided tours and a museum.

Website: http://www.indianamuseum.org
Address: 202 East Walnut Street, Corydon, Indiana
Phone: (812) 738-4890.

KENTUCKY SIDE

Owensboro

Josiah Henson Trail

There is a twelve-mile section of US 60 that is designated as the Josiah Henson Trail, from Owensboro to the Josiah Henson Historical Marker. (Slightly three miles east of the split from Maceo and US 231.) The marker

The Lincoln Boyhood Home interprets Lincoln's early years and life on the Ohio River near Evansville. *Courtesy of Kaitlyn Dickerson.*

Josiah Henson Historical Marker on US Highway 60 outside of Owensboro marks the Riley Farm where Henson was enslaved with his family. This is the farm from which they escaped to Canada. *Author's collection.*

is on the south side of US 60 and is easy to miss. There is no pullover, and the highway is very busy, but it is good to note the location of the Riley Farm where Henson lived and escaped from with his family. The marker is in a wooded stretch of road on both sides and is titled "Uncle Tom Lived Here."

The Bluegrass Music Hall of Fame and Museum

The Bluegrass Music Hall of Fame and Museum is a cultural center dedicated to protecting, preserving and promoting bluegrass music. A couple of exhibits examine river music and the history of blues with contributions from African Americans. There are concerts throughout the year in the Woodward Theatre.

Website: www.bluegrasshall.org
Address: 311 West Second Street, Owensboro, Kentucky
Phone: (270) 926-7891

Owensboro Courthouse, Waterfront and Strother Playground

There are historical markers and statues on the courthouse lawn in the center of town. A marker is dedicated to the U.S. Daviess County Colored Troops who mustered in at the site. Another historical marker explains the destruction of courthouses in Kentucky from Rebel forces. The statue

The Bluegrass Music Hall of Fame and Museum has exhibits on origins of bluegrass music with tributes to African Americans. Special concerts are held throughout the year. *Author's collection*.

The Owensboro waterfront features Strother's Park, an extensive waterpark to relax and enjoy river views and a play area for children. The courthouse yard is located nearby with historic markers on African Americans and the Civil War. *Author's collection*.

of a pink pig, Chester, gives a nod to the area's well-known reputation for southern barbeque. The Strother Playground and river walkway is just a couple of blocks away. The playground is one of the nicest along the Ohio River. It has a natural history theme with giant trees, birds and fish that kids can play in and around. It also has nice restrooms and a picnic area.

Brandenburg

Located upriver between Owensboro and Louisville, Brandenburg is best known as the actual crossing site of General John Hunt Morgan and his 2,400 Confederate raiders who wreaked havoc through the southern borders of Indiana and Ohio before their capture. There is a park by the river at Brandenburg with a statue commemorating Confederate general John Hunt Morgan and his raiders. The statue *Freedom*, by Louisville sculptor Wyatt Gragg, honors the area as a site on the UGRR. The same statue was created for the Freedom Center in Cincinnati and is located in the lobby.

Nearby, there were crossing areas at various points on the UGRR at Leavenworth, Mauckport and Morvins Landing, but specific locations are not known and are only found through oral histories. From there, places such as Bill Crawford's farm, near Corydon, was a well-sought refuge for fugitives traveling north. Information about a well-known fugitive slave case, the Brandenburg Affair, can be found online at www.genealogytrails. com. The trail is not well marked, but it is significant enough for mention.

LOUISVILLE'S SLAVE TRADE

Louisville, Kentucky, and New Albany, Clarksville and Jeffersonville, Indiana

L ouisville's position on the river was important in the antebellum years because the Falls of the Ohio was a significant interruption in the river traffic. Before the Portland Canal was constructed in 1830, flatboats and steamboats had to offload their cargo above the falls, carry it below the falls and reload it back on the boat.[26] The falls location made this operation take place on the Kentucky side of the river, creating a stopping point for all commercial operations, which resulted in hotels, taverns, ship suppliers, builders and many other businesses that began to depend on river traffic. The mercantile and shipbuilding trades became aggressive and profitable.

With the creation of the Portland Canal, the first canal built on the Ohio River, in 1830, Louisville became the "focus of Ohio River steam-boating. In 1829, more than 1,000 steamboats landed at Louisville—300 more than at New Orleans and ten times more than at Pittsburgh."[27] In 1846, the Louisville Directory recorded that 1,626 steamboats and 283 flat- and keelboats passed through the Louisville and Portland Canals with 341,695 tons of cargo generating $149,401.81 in tolls. Louisville improved and graded the wharf areas to meet the demands of regulating all of this traffic, which was an important part of commerce for the region. Louisville placed limits of forty-eight hours for a boat's stay and "instructed the harbor master to auction off vessels that exceeded the limit."[28] How much of that "cargo" accounted for human trafficking is not known.

The steamboat-building industry became an important trade on the Ohio River because merchants could build boats locally and cheaper than

The Portland Canal became an important shipping port for Louisville and connected fugitive slaves to the UGRR in New Albany. *98.11.055. Furnas Family Album, Archives and Special Collections, University of Louisville.*

the shipyards on the coastal areas. The Howard family began an inland shipbuilding industry in the 1830s in Jeffersonville, Indiana, and continued running it through much of the twentieth century. The shipyards were purchased by Jeffboat, which continued building inland ships until its recent closure.

Steamboats and shipyards required a lot of raw materials, such as timber, fuel (timber and later coal) and iron (for engines). Not only did the steamboat-manufacturing industry require a lot of resources, the logistics for moving the shipments of goods and commodities was a big business. The following shows the magnitude of goods imported from the Ohio River at the Louisville shipyard in 1860:

> *A Table of Imports Per River: June 1860*
> *773 Casks of Bacon, 536 Pieces of Bagging, 412 Coils of Rope, 34 Bales Twine, 2399 Bales Hemp, 372 Bales Cotton, 1146 Bags Cotton Yarns, 490 Bales Cotton Batting, 195 Boxes Imported Candles, 845 Boxes Cheese, 1301 Bags Coffee, 350000 Bushels Coal, 13615 Boxes*

Dry Goods, 3575 Pkgs. Drugs, 1146 Bags Wheat, 4173 Bags Corn, 915 Bags Oats, 24 Barrels Lard, 48 Kegs Lard, 244 Heads of Hogs, 5123 Boxes Glass, 99 Crates and Casks, 1353 Bales Hay, 626 Bundles of Hides, 4157 Barrels of Flour, 3908 Barrels of Whiskey, 3511 Kegs Nails, 5782 Pieces Iron, 1834 Bundles Iron, 492 Tons of Pig Iron, 6720 Bundles of Paper, 124 Pkg. Flax Seed, 75000 Shingles, 387 Hhds Sugar, 1293 Barrels Sugar, 446 Lead pigs, 1371 Kegs White Lead, 860 Boxes Tin, 550 Barrels Molasses, 98 Half Barrels Molasses, 73 Bags Shot, 75 Barrels Tar, 10 Kegs Tar, 1557 Hhds Tobacco, 836 Boxes Tobacco, 124 Barrels Turpentine, 286 Barrels Liquor, 323 Boxes Liquor, 220 Bales Oakum, 235 Barrels Mackerel, 455 Pkgs. Mackerel, 3943 T.L. Salt, 25 Half Chests of Tea, 74 Pkgs. Tea, 296 Bags Wool, 75 Pkgs. Spices, 116 Tierces Rice, 795 Bags Meal, 4413 Bags of Bran and Shorts.[29]

All of these ventures—spin-off industries and commercial and mercantile associations—created a need for a workforce, and slave "bondsmen" became a source of hire-outs to provide that workforce. Slaveholders would place their slaves into well paying positions, including hemp and tobacco production, iron furnaces (for producing steam engines), gristmills, woolen mills, nail factories. Some owners allowed their slaves to be hired out to businesses that allowed both owners and slaves to be paid. The steamboat industry in Louisville was no exception. Slaves worked in all aspects of the shipyard, as draymen, stevedores, machinists, dockworkers and runners, and on the boats themselves, as deck mates, chambermaids, cooks and musicians. Slaves "preferred to lease themselves because it gave them leverage for increasing their independence. Hiring one's own time frequently meant association with free blacks or even living in a free black community."[30]

Placing slaves with commission agents and slave traders for leasing was another form of renting out slaves, especially in Kentucky's larger cities like Louisville. Some agents hired slaves for clients or for speculations. One Louisville firm, preparing for a new year's demand for labor, advertised, "100 women and boys for brick-yards, draymen, etc. 40 men and boys for ropewalks, 40 men and boys for hotel waiters, and 50 boys and girls for tobacco stemmeries."[31]

THE SLAVE JAILS AND SLAVE MARKETS IN LOUISVILLE

By the mid-nineteenth century, Louisville had become the largest city along the Ohio River for slave trafficking, with slave traders holding slaves until shipments were large enough to be shipped to supply the southern markets.[32] These slave traders, bounty hunters, slave owners and auctioneers were very visible and operated their businesses between the blocks of First and Sixth Streets and Main and Jefferson Streets, in proximity to the river.

Slave sales took place under a variety of conditions. Some auctioneers would auction an individual with a classified ad to meet at a certain time and date on the street corner. Slave buyers boldly announced wanted ads for 250 to 300 "negroes," male and female, at top market prices. Others placed ads for runaways with descriptions of certain features of the individuals. In addition to private slave jails owned by slave traders, the city jail would "hold slaves," particularly those who had been caught as runaways. If no owner appeared for claim, the slave would be dealt with "as law requires," meaning held for public auction. Jailors and courts would be paid in addition for holding slaves in confinement. The system of slavery included traders, owners and elected and appointed officials, including sheriffs, deputy sheriffs, posses, justices of the peace and appointed local militias.

In the following, Henry Bibb describes the Louisville jail workhouse where he, his wife and daughter lived for three months before being shipped to New Orleans:

> I had not been in this prison many days before Madison [Mathew] Garrison, the soul driver, bought me and my family to sell in the New Orleans slave market. He was buying up slaves to take to New Orleans. So he took me and my little family to the work-house, to be kept under lock and key at work until he had bought up as many as he wished to take off to the South.
>
> The work-house of Louisville was a very large brick building, built on the plan of a jail or State's prison, with many apartments to it, divided off into cells wherein prisoners were locked up after night, the upper apartments were occupied by females, principally. This prison was enclosed by a high stone wall, upon which stood watchman with loaded guns to guard the prisoners from breaking out, and on either side there were large iron gates…. When the large iron gate or door was thrown open to receive us, it was astonishing to see so many whites as well as colored men loaded down with irons, at hard labor, under the supervision of overseers…

Want ads like this one from June 30, 1860, appeared frequently in the *Louisville Daily Democrat. Microfilm, Louisville Free Public Library*.

    The people of color who were in there were slaves there without crime but for safe keeping, while the whites were some of the most abandoned characters living. The keeper took me up to the anvil block and fastened a chain about my leg, which I had to drag after me both day and night during three months. My labor was sawing stone; my food was coarse corn bread and beef shanks and cows heads with pot liquor, and a very scanty allowance of that.

    I have often seen meat spoiled when brought to us, covered with flies and fly blows, and even worms crawling over it, when we were compelled

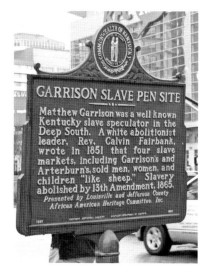

PRISON, LOUISVILLE, KY.

Left: The Garrison Slave Pen historical marker, located on Main Street in Louisville, is only one of the many slave jails in this vicinity between First and Sixth Streets and Main and Jefferson Streets. *Author's collection.*

Right: Sketch of the Louisville jail, which was the typical architecture for jails in that time period. It featured a castle and moat type of presence. *Lewis Collins, 1850, Historical Sketches of Kentucky.*

> *to eat it, or go without any at all. It was all spread out on a long table in separate plates; and at the sound of a bell, every one would take his plate, asking no questions.*

THE FREE BLACK COMMUNITY IN LOUISVILLE AND THE UNDERGROUND RAILROAD

In 1840, there were 26,987 white people living in the Louisville/Jefferson County area, with 763 free blacks and 8,596 slaves.[33] Being a free black in a slave city had many problems, as described by Louisvillian Washington Spradling (1803–68):

> *Our principal difficulty here grows out of the police laws, which are very stringent. For instance, a police officer may go [to] a house at night, without any search warrant, and, if the door is not opened when he knocks, force it in, and ransack the house, and the colored man has no redress. At other*

times, they come and say they are hunting for stolen goods or for runaway slaves, and, some of them being great scoundrels, if they see a piece of goods, which may have been purchased, they will take it and carry it off. If I go out of the state, I cannot come back to it again. The penalty is imprisonment in the penitentiary....My children are just tied down here. If they go to Louisiana, there is no chance for them, unless I can get some white to go to New Orleans and swear they belong to him, and claim them as his slaves. As I understand it, a freeman cannot get permission to go to the state and come back.[34]

Washington Spradling was a prominent man in Louisville and perhaps the wealthiest black at the time. W.H. Gibson describes Spradling:

The leading colored man in business and the largest real estate holder. He was a barber by trade but he made his mark as a business man by trading and brokerage, in connection with his shaving. His mode of making money consisted in buying and leasing lots in different parts of the city and building and moving frame cottages upon those lots. He also built several brick business houses on Third Street. Mr. Spradling had many peculiarities; his dress was very common, as he exhibited no pride in that direction. He loved to converse on law, and thought he was uneducated, was considered one of the best lawyers to plan or prepare a case for the court. He was very successful, and nearly every colored person who was in trouble more or less, consulted with Washington Spradling. He selected the lawyer and prepared the case. He was seldom defeated, and if so, he was sure to take an appeal. His customers were the first judges and lawyers of the State, and from long and constant contact with them he seemed to have acquired their inspiration. He was a Methodist by profession being a member of the Jackson Street M.E. Church.

Spradling was also a conductor on the UGRR. "Wash Spradley [*sic*] a shrew negro, was instrumental in helping many his enslaved brethren out of bondage."[35] In one case published in the *National Anti-Slavery Standard*, well-known conductor Calvin Fairbanks described shaking hands with Washington Spradling at the "Centre Street Church for colored persons... where Bird Parker preaches" before the disappearance of Tamar, a young slave woman. Fairbank was successful in ferreting Tamar on a skiff to Jeffersonville and then onto a train at Salem.[36] In an interview, Spradling stated, "I have bought thirty-three other slaves, a good many of whom have repaid me, and a good many have not. There is now $3337.50 due me from slaves that I have purchased."[37]

Shelton Morris was the brother-in-law of Washington Spradling and established a barbershop and bathhouse under the old Galt House. Together, they purchased real estate that became the Russell neighborhood, often called Louisville's Harlem. Morris moved to Cincinnati in 1841 and became a well-known operator for the Underground Railroad, according to Levi Coffin.[38] Eliza Curtis Hundley Tevis was another free black who purchased a large area of land, which was developed into the Newburg/Petersburg community. She also purchased slaves and emancipated them.[39]

In his autobiography, W.H. Gibson describes life in antebellum Louisville, detailing how the black community worked together for the education and religious training of free and enslaved blacks. Gibson was a free black, born in Baltimore, who had education and training in music. In 1847, he moved to Louisville and opened a day-and-night school, initially in a small colored church behind Fifth Street Baptist. In the early 1850s, he organized a special choir of children, the Union Singing School, supported by colored churches Quinn Chapel, Center Street and Jackson Street Methodist Episcopal.

The Quinn Chapel AME was connected to other AME congregations in Indiana and Ohio. The church began as the Bethel House of God on Second and Main Streets, across from the old Galt House. Bishop Paul Quinn was said to have preached from a boat in the Ohio River because it was not safe for him to land in Kentucky. His voice carried over the water to the people who congregate on the shore. It received support from Quaker organizations and was no doubt involved in the UGRR. By the 1850s there were eight independent black churches in Louisville, and most were involved in the education of both free and enslaved blacks.

The Green Street Baptist Church began under the leadership of Pastor George Wells in 1844, as the Second Colored Baptist Church, with permission of slave owners from Walnut Street Baptist Church. Slaves walked from plantations along Newburg Road, carrying their shoes, meeting first at Third and Green Streets, then at a livery stable on Green between Preston and Floyd Streets. This church has been involved in the civil rights movement, and in 1967, it hosted a citywide rally to encourage blacks to register and vote. Dr. Martin Luther King Jr. spoke and made his last appearance in Louisville at this rally.

Besides giving a detailed history of the black churches in Louisville before the Civil War, Gibson described the formation of the first black Masonic organization in the area. The warrant for a lodge in Louisville

Right: Business leader and UGRR conductor Washington Spradling is buried in Eastern Cemetery. Spradling was instrumental in helping blacks with legal issues in Louisville courts. *Author's collection.*

Below: The Green Street Baptist Church at 519 East Gray Street in Louisville was organized in 1844 under the leadership of Pastor George Wells and has been a leader in civil rights since that time. Martin Luther King Jr. led a rally here in 1967 to encourage blacks to vote. *Author's collection.*

for free blacks was met with prejudice, so a warrant was secured from Cincinnati, and the Mount Moriah Lodge was formed in 1850 across the river in New Albany, Indiana.[40]

By the Civil War, thousands of slave fugitives had fled to Louisville to join the Union army. By 1864, one hundred blacks enlisted each day at the Taylor Barracks at Third and Oak Streets and became members of regiments of U.S. Colored Troops 107th, 108th, 109th, 122th, 123th and 125th. At the war's end approximately twenty-four thousand black Kentuckians had served in the Union army amid the threats of hostile whites and dangers on the battlefields.

THE FIRST RIOT IN DETROIT: THE BLACKBURNS

The Blackburn historical marker on Main Street by the Galt House cites the Lucie and Thorton Blackburn escape to Detroit. Attempts to extradite them back to Kentucky resulted in Detroit's first race riot. *Author's collection.*

Thorton Blackburn was a slave from Mason County who was sold and ended up in Louisville. He met his wife, Lucie, in Louisville, and they escaped by boat to Detroit, Michigan, in 1831. In 1833, slave catchers from Kentucky went to Detroit and arrested the couple and jailed them in Detroit before taking them back to Kentucky.

The Blackburns were allowed to have visitors in Detroit, which gave Lucie the opportunity to exchange clothes with a visitor and then escape to Canada. Thorton was shackled, so his escape was more difficult, but the day before he was to be returned to Louisville, a crowd of four hundred men stormed the jail, allowing Blackburn to escape. The commotion turned into a two-day riot during which a local sheriff was shot and killed. This was the first race riot in the United States and resulted in the formation of the Riot Commission. Thorton was pursued as he fled north and was able to board a boat to Canada where he met his wife.[41]

NEW ALBANY

The most important crossing point in the greater Louisville area was located west of Portland-leading from Louisville across the Ohio River to New Albany.[42] Associations of free blacks in New Albany and their likely assistance to help refugees, both through the Masonic lodge and churches, was instrumental in helping fugitive slaves.[43] The most important crossing point in the Greater Louisville area was from the Portland Canal, directly across from New Albany. This crossing was corroborated by interviews taken from the Federal Writers Project, initiated through the Works Progress Administration in the 1930s, which included oral histories about the UGRR from families. Sarah Merrill's great uncle Lewis Barnett said he and twelve others crossed the river at Portland, then went over to New Albany, down Cherry Street and up to the Knobs. He said there was a colored Masonic lodge in Portland that helped plan escapes.[44]

Many of these escapes used the railroads, both to follow the rail as a trail and to board trains, which at that time included the New Albany and Chicago Railroad and the Madison and Indianapolis Railroad. There were three main routes—one from Cincinnati; one from Madison, Indiana; and one from Jeffersonville, Indiana, across from Louisville—fugitives followed from the Ohio River, which converged at the home of Levi and Catherine "Aunt Katie" Coffin in Newport, Indiana (now Fountain City). Levi Coffin was deemed the Father of the Underground Railroad. The Coffins lived in their home in Newport for twenty years, then moved to Cincinnati in 1847. It is estimated that three thousand fugitive slaves were under their protection. Not a single one was captured while under the care of the Coffins during those years in Newport and Cincinnati.[45]

Levi Coffin wrote about a white man named Jones who aided runaway slaves in Louisville whenever possible. He would purchase a stateroom on the Louisville to Cincinnati packet boat, and he would get a key to the room. Shortly before the boat left the dock, among the hustle and bustle along the wharf, he would have fugitives bring on large bundles, as if carrying baggage for their owners, and, with a prearranged signal, the fugitives would go to the stateroom and lock the door. Jones would sometimes accompany the group. Packet boats left Louisville early in the morning and would reach Cincinnati before daylight the next day. Coffin was waiting for the boat to arrive in Cincinnati and would arrange for a person to go onboard and help the fugitives off the boat, usually unnoticed

Lucie Higgs Nichols, an escaped slave living in New Albany, served as a nurse during the Civil War. Here (*second row, center*) she is pictured with the veterans of the Twenty-Third Indiana Volunteer Infantry. It is part of the exhibit at the permanent exhibit *Ordinary People, Extraordinary Courage: Men and Women of the Underground Railroad* at the Carnegie Center for Art and History in New Albany. *Courtesy of the Carnegie Center for Art and History.*

amid the "crowd of colored porters, draymen and hackmen."[46] Coffin recalled that one spring and summer, twenty-seven fugitives escaped this way from Louisville to Cincinnati.

The Louisville area became an odd mix of free and enslaved blacks, where the distinction between the two blurred among the hustle and bustle of a city, enabling more opportunities for fugitives to make for an effective escape.

SCENIC BYWAYS

River Road on Kentucky side: Take River Road for ten miles from the wharf area in downtown Louisville (by Belle of Louisville) to US 42 in Prospect. Includes waterfront, the Louisville Water Tower and Locust Grove.

Ohio Scenic Byway: This continues through Indiana and Ohio. For more information: www.ohioriverbyway.com/maps.

PLACES TO VISIT

INDIANA SIDE

New Albany

Albany began settlement in 1817 and quickly became known for riverboat building and glass manufacturing. John B. Ford's New Albany Glass Works produced and installed the first plate glass windows in the United States. One of the first railroads in the area, later known as Monon Railroad, connected New Albany to Salem, Indiana. There was a small free black neighborhood here that was active in the UGRR during the Civil War. New Albany became a strategic supply center for the Union army and a hospital center for the wounded.

The city has preserved many of its historic buildings and offers walkways along the river, restaurants, museums. The Horseshoe Casino is nearby.

Town Clock Church

The Town Clock Church stands out as a "beacon of hope" as it rises above other historic buildings in this Indiana community. The church was built by the Second Presbyterians, who were led by known antislavery ministers such as Reverend Samuel K. Sneed, Reverend John Guest Atterbury

and Reverend John Bishop, who had affiliations with abolitionist groups. Reverend Bishop was a graduate of the Lane Seminary in Cincinnati, which was an important institution in the antislavery movement (discussed in more detail in chapter 4). The church, which also had black members, formed aid societies to help blacks in the community.[47] Today the church operates as the Second Baptist Church. Visitors can walk around the

Old Town Clock Church stands out in the landscape of New Albany and was a part of the UGGR. *Author's collection.*

church and see the garden and sculpture area with more interpretive signage. The church is open during church services.

Website: www.townclockchurch.org
Address: 300 East Main Street, New Albany, Indiana

Carnegie Center for Art and History

Carnegie is a site on the National Park Service National Underground Railroad Network with a permanent hands-on exhibit, "Ordinary People, Extraordinary Courage," which focuses on the local contributions of people who challenged the institution of slavery. The exhibit is highlighted by an interactive feature-length multimedia film. The center also has temporary exhibits, sponsors workshops, talks and events throughout the year. The museum is closed on Sunday and Monday.

Website: www.carnegiecenter.org
Address: 201 East Spring Street, New Albany, Indiana
Phone: (812) 944-7336

Falls of the Ohio Interpretive Center

A beautiful interpretive center overlooks this series of rapids that drop twenty-four feet over a two-mile stretch on the Ohio River. This marked the stopping point for people traveling along the Ohio River, with Louisville on the south side and Clarksville and New Albany on the north side. It marked the rise of the steamboat trade in Louisville that also gave Louisville the distinction of the slave trafficking center for southern slave markets. The center sits on a small bluff overlooking a large sweep of the Ohio River, including a waterfall dam and Louisville. In dry summer months, naturalists lead groups across large fossil beds that expose the bones and fossils of ancient marine life that thrived here during the Devonian Period. With hands-on cultural and natural history exhibits, the interpretive center operates as an Indiana State Park. There is an admission charge.

Website: www.fallsoftheohio.org
Address: 201 West Riverside Drive, Clarksville, Indiana
Phone: (812) 280-9970

The Carnegie Center for Art and History Museum is a designation on the National Park Service National Underground Railroad Network. *Author's collection.*

The Falls of the Ohio Museum offers breathtaking views of the Falls of the Ohio and includes extensive exhibits on the history and natural history of the Ohio River. *Author's collection.*

Jeffersonville

Howard Steamboat Museum

James Howard began his shipbuilding in 1834 on a fifty-two-acre area on the north shore of the Ohio River, in Jeffersonville, Indiana, across from Louisville. His first boat, *The Hyperion* was launched, and the business continued throughout the nineteenth and early twentieth centuries. In 1894, James's son, Edward, built the twenty-two-room mansion that serves as the museum today. The Howard Shipyards became Jeffboat by World War II and built more than one hundred landing ship tanks. Jeffboat was the largest inland shipbuilder in the United States until its recent closure. The Howard Steamboat Museum has models and displays that share the history of the steamboat era in the United States. There are daily tours, and it is five minutes from downtown Louisville.

Website: www.howardsteamboatmuseum.org
Address: 1101 East Market Street, Jeffersonville, Indiana
Phone: (812) 283-3728

KENTUCKY SIDE

Louisville

Main Street and Belvedere, Downtown Louisville

The areas between First and Sixth Streets and Main and Jefferson Streets are the sites where slave traders operated. Many of the sites had private slaveholding jails—there are two markers for slave trade sites and one marker designating Blackburn slave escape. Today Main Street is known for its beautifully preserved cast iron–façade buildings and the newly constructed KFC Yum! Center, home of the University of Louisville basketball teams. The *Belle of Louisville* steamboat and her sister ship, the *Mary M. Miller*, is docked along part of the original wharf.

The York Statue is located on Riverfront Plaza Belvedere (by the Galt House Hotel, overlooking the river) between Main Street and the river. York was a famous African American explorer from the Corps of Discovery Expedition (1804–1806). On several occasions, he was responsible for the safety of the corps, in rescues, acquisition of food and interactions with

Above: The Howard Steamboat Museum in Jeffersonville explores the history of the Howard family who settled in the Louisville area in the 1830s and became major steamboat builders through the early twentieth century. *Author's collection.*

Right: The York statue on the Belvedere in downtown Louisville by the Muhammed Ali Museum gives tribute to York, who was enslaved by Meriwether Lewis. York was responsible for the safety and survival of the Lewis and Clark expedition in several cases. *Author's collection.*

Native Americans. Enslaved by William Clark, York's fate is not known. York and William Clark had a "falling-out," and Clark hired York out to a farmer in Louisville after Clark had moved to Missouri. The story ends there with little known of York's later years.

Museum Row on Main Street

The Muhammed Ali Center has exhibits on various aspects of history that deal with human trafficking, civil rights, freedom and slavery. The area is also home to the Louisville Slugger Museum and Factory, Frazier Museum, Evan Williams Bourbon Experience, KMAC Museum, Peerless Distilling Company and Louisville Science Center. The Frazier Museum has bourbon trail information and highlights some contributions from African Americans to Kentucky commodities. In addition, they have various temporary exhibits throughout the year.

Website: www.fraziermuseum.org
Address: 829 West Main Street, Louisville, Kentucky
Phone: (502) 753-5663

The Muhammed Ali Museum examines Ali's life and his contributions to civil rights. Many displays and hands-on activities connect civil rights history to modern day. *Author's collection.*

The Ali museum provides a valuable link forward from emancipation to the civil rights movement by examining Muhmmed Ali's life. Interactive exhibits and updated information demonstrate the continued issue of human trafficking and human rights violations today. Both museums have admission charges.

Website: www.alicenter.org
Address: 144 North Sixth Street, Louisville, Kentucky
Phone: (502) 584-9254.

Kentucky Center for African American Heritage

The center is located in the 1876 Louisville Street Railway Complex for the City of Louisville. It has a small number of exhibits on local African Americans. It is an event center and conducts various programs throughout the year. The center is closed on weekends. There is an admission charge.

Website: www.kcaah.org
Address: 1701 West Muhammed Ali Boulevard, Louisville, Kentucky
Phone: (502) 582-4100

Belle of Louisville **Riverboat and Wharf Area**

To experience the magnificence and craftmanship of the steamboat era, a trip on the *Belle of Louisville* can transport you back in time. The *Belle of Louisville* was built in Pittsburgh and made its maiden voyage in 1914. Even though it was made a half century after the Civil War, its style and structure are much the same as the antebellum boats. Its sturdy frame was built on top of a steel hull that needed only five feet of water to float, giving it flexibility to navigate almost any type of river. Its original name was *Idlewild* and it spent its early years as a passenger ferry between Memphis and West Memphis, though it also hauled cargo like lumber and cotton. In 1931, it was purchased by the Rose Island Company in Louisville to ferry passengers fourteen miles upriver from Louisville to the Rose Island Amusement Park. The park closed after the 1937 flood.

During World War II, the *Idlewild* served many purposes, including as a floating nightclub for the United Service Organizations to entertain troops. The *Idlewild* was purchased by investors in Cincinnati in 1947 and was named *The Avalon*. It spent the next thirteen years as the most widely

The *Belle of Louisville* is a way to experience an authentic paddle wheeler and steamboat from the past on the Ohio River. The *Belle* and its sister ship, *Mary M. Miller*, offer daily voyages throughout the year. *Author's collection.*

traveled river steamer in the nation. In 1962, Jefferson County judge Dave Armstrong purchased *The Avalon*, bringing it back to Louisville where it was renamed the *Belle of Louisville*. Since that time, it has become the "host" of Louisville, taking millions of visitors back in time by offering daily ventures on the Ohio River. Docked at the Louisville wharf, it is the oldest steamboat in operation. There are many special events, as well as lunch and evening cruises throughout the year.

Website: www.belleoflouisville.org
Phone: (866) 832-0011

Louisville Waterfront Park

This beautifully designed eighty-five-acre public park is open daily from 6:00 a.m. to 11:00 p.m. It includes the *Belle of Louisville* wharf area and extends eastward past the Big Four Bridge that crosses into Jeffersonville, Indiana. The pedestrian and bicycle bridge allows a unique view of the Ohio River, providing a sense of perspective about the Louisville waterfront and its

Waterfront Park is a great way to experience the Ohio River with scenic views and activities such as a playground and spray park. There is a pedestrian walkway over the river to Jeffersonville, which has a lot of eateries and shops. *Author's collection.*

historic presence. Walkers are treated to various restaurants, eateries and bars on the Jeffersonville, Indiana, side. The park also includes a large playground with a spray park. There are many sculptures, such as *Flock of Finns* by local artist Marvin Finn and *Lincoln Memorial* by Ed Hamilton. The Louisville Slugger Field, home of the professional minor league team the Louisville Bats, which is a Triple-A affiliate of the Cincinnati Reds, is located nearby.

Jefferson County—Louisville area

President Zachary Taylor Cemetery Gravesite at the Zachary Taylor National Cemetery

There is an unmarked area beside President Zachary Taylor's grave, which is known as a burial site of slaves from the Taylor family.[48] Many Taylors settled in the Louisville and Oldham County areas, almost all of whom were slaveholders. President Zachary Taylor's historic home is located within a block of the cemetery and is a private residence that has been gracefully preserved. A historic marker stands near the home. It is open daily from sunrise to sunset.

Address: 4701 Brownsboro Road, Louisville, Kentucky
Phone: (502) 893-3852

Farmington Historic Home

Farmington was a hemp plantation owned by John and Lucy Speed. The Speeds had large slaveholdings to work on hemp production. The Speed's son, Joshua, was close friend of Abraham Lincoln. Lincoln visited the home and wrote bread and butter letters to Mrs. Speed, one of which contains Lincoln's observations of slaves chained on a boat going down to the Ohio River to southern slave markets. It is a beautifully preserved historic home and museum with interpretive exhibits, daily house tours, planned activities throughout the year and documented slave escapes. It is open daily, except holidays. There is an admission charge.

Website: www.farmingtonhistoricplantation.org
Address: 3033 Bardstown Road, Louisville, Kentucky
Phone: (502) 452-9920.

Locust Grove

Founded in 1790, Locust Grove was the home of William and Lucy Clark Croghan. Lucy was the sister of surveyor George Rogers Clark and William Clark of the Lewis and Clark expedition. George Rogers Clark lived at Locust Grove from 1809 until his death in 1818. William Clark and his friend Meriwether Lewis led the Corps of Discovery Expedition, which was the first American expedition to cross the western portion of the United States. Expedition members stayed at the Croghan home several times. William Clark brought his slave York on the expedition. York became well-known for his bravery handling firearms, killing game and navigating waterways and trails. The hands-on museum includes information on the lives of enslaved people and daily tours of the well-preserved historic home and slave outbuildings, as well as trails and planned activities throughout the year. Locust Grove is located about half a mile off the Ohio River Road Scenic Byway. There is an admission charge.

Website: www.locustgrove.org
Address: 561 Blankenbaker Lane, Louisville, Kentucky

Riverside: The Farnsley-Moremen Landing in Western Jefferson County

The Farnsley-Mormen House (circa 1837) is the centerpiece of a three-hundred-acre site on the Ohio River called Riverside. From 1820 until

Farmington Historic Plantation is the beautifully preserved home of the Speed family, who were slave holders and hemp farmers. There are recorded slave escapes here. Abraham Lincoln visited this home that now offers daily tours of the grounds. *Author's collection.*

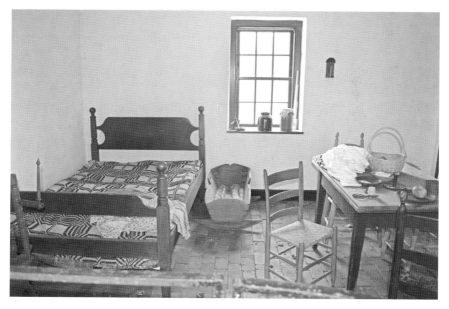

This slave cabin (built circa 1792) is one of the many buildings restored at Locust Grove. This remaining fifty-five-acre tract of William and Lucy Clark Groghan's estate is an excellent example of life in antebellum Louisville. This is a hands-on museum with exhibits on slavery and many restored buildings. It has daily tours, a gift shop and special events throughout the year. *Author's collection.*

1890, it had an active riverboat landing used by the families to transport goods and provide fuel for boats. This mimicked other landings that could be found up and down the river during those years. There was also a ferry that operated to connect Kentucky and Indiana. Both the Farnsleys and Moremans were slaveholders. It has daily tours, archaeology programs and a museum.

Website: www.riverside-landing.org
Address: 7410 Moorman Road, Louisville, Kentucky
Phone: (502) 935-6809

3

THE SHALLOWS TO MADISON

Madison and Vevay, Indiana, and Westport, Bedford, LaGrange, Milton, Carrollton and Warsaw, Kentucky

By 1849, the Madison and Indianapolis Railroad had just been completed, making Madison, Indiana, the gateway to distribute all the "northbound produce" from the Ohio River to the "capital and surrounding areas."[49] Nestled between Louisville and Cincinnati, the rich bottomland along the river and the vast stores of trees (fuel for steamboats) made the town ideal for steam and packet boat stops.

The UGRR system between Oldham, Trimble and Carroll County along the river in Kentucky to Madison in Jefferson County, Indiana was very well known. As a place for crossing, the point of the river at Madison is shallow and narrow. During the nineteenth century, there were many times when the river was so low it was only four feet deep. People could wade, swim and ride horseback across the river, particularly where sandbars were present. There were also deep ravines along creek beds on both sides of the river that allowed people to follow northern routes.[50]

Steamboats and keelboats could stop at the many small landings along both sides of the Ohio River. The Oldham County Historical Society listed forty-nine river ports or landings between Louisville and Milton, Kentucky (across from Madison), on both sides in the nineteenth century.[51] Each landing became a direct connection for farmers to send their produce and products to larger towns. Many of the larger plantations had their own landing. These landings were in continuous use well after the Civil War and through the middle of the twentieth century. The landings provided ways to gather slaves from rural communities and take them to larger ports, such as Louisville, and then to southern slave markets, but the landings also provided an escape route for freedom seekers to hop on packets and boats undetected.

THE GEORGETOWN DISTRICT

In the late 1700s, some families, upset with the culture of slavery in Kentucky and Louisville, moved to the Madison area.[52] These antislavery families gave support to blacks who were actively working to strengthen support for runaway slaves. The Georgetown District in Madison was a black neighborhood with forty-eight families listed in the 1820s, growing to almost three hundred by the mid-1850s. There were small black communities close by in Graysville and Hanover. During the 1830s and '40s, UGRR conductors in the area included George DeBaptiste (1815–1875), Elijah Anderson (1808–1861), Chapman Harris (1802–1890) and William Anderson (1811–1867).

DeBaptiste was an important figure and leader on the UGRR and in the antislavery movement. Born free in Virginia, he worked in the steamboat business as a young man. DeBaptiste moved to Madison around 1836 and invested in local businesses. In 1840, DeBaptiste served as a valet and White House steward for President William Henry Harrison (who was from Indiana). After Harrison's death, (from pneumonia thirty-one days into his term), DeBaptiste returned to Madison and opened his barbershop, which became the operating center of the Madison UGRR. His operation included the assistance of the Levi and Catherine Coffin. The Coffins' home in Newport, Indiana, had become a major refuge center for runaway slaves, earning Levi Coffin the title of Father of the Underground Railroad. After civil unrest and violence in Madison, DeBaptiste moved to Detroit and connected with other abolitionist and UGRR workers, such as Henry Bibb. In Detroit, he operated a steamship that ferried fugitives from Detroit to Canada and continued working on many causes for blacks until his death.

Elijah Anderson also risked his life to help fugitives, and he paid the price. He ran a blacksmith shop in Madison and, in his narrative written in later years, described assisting eighteen hundred fugitives. He often used the mouth of the Kentucky River in Carrollton as a key crossing to assist slaves.[53] Anderson moved his blacksmith business upriver to Lawrenceburg, Indiana, and continued to help fugitives cross the river. In his final act assisting twelve

UGRR conductor Elijah Anderson's house (*right*) is one of the restored homes in historic Georgetown District, which was an African American neighborhood that was important on the UGRR in Madison. *Author's collection.*

fugitives, he was caught and sentenced to an eight-year term in the Kentucky penitentiary at Frankfort. On the day he was to be released, March 4, 1861, he was found dead in his cell.

Chapman Harris, a free black, arrived in Madison in 1837 and stayed there for the rest of his life. He remained in spite of mob violence that threatened and drove others away. Harris lived on a high ridge called Eagle Hollow one mile east of Madison. He was a minister and a blacksmith and was jailed and suffered numerous threats and mistreatment, but he still continued to work to help others escape.

Harris used an anvil placed in the trunk of a sycamore tree as a signal that he or his sons were ready to row across the river to pick up fugitives in Kentucky. He would hammer on the anvil as a notice to fugitives and other agents in the area.

The fugitives who fled to Madison came through Oldham, Trimble and Carroll Counties, which bordered the Kentucky side of the Ohio River. Milton (in Trimble County) was small milltown directly across from Madison. Hunter's Bottom, by Milton, was an area composed of wealthy slaveholders who held estates overlooking the river.

Trimble County was created in 1836 from portions of Oldham and Henry Counties, and Bedford, in Trimble County, became the county seat. Henry Bibb, born in 1815 in Henry County, eventually lived at the William Gatewood plantation near Bedford, where he was enslaved with his wife, Malinda, and daughter, Mary Frances. Westport, in Oldham County (formed in 1824), was located on the river and was the county seat, but the county seat moved inland to LaGrange in 1838. At the time when Bibb and his family lived on the Gatewood plantation, it was a part of Oldham County. William Gatewood was very involved in Oldham County politics before Trimble County was formed.

ELEUTHERIAN COLLEGE

Eleutherian College was built ten miles from Madison and four miles south of Dupont on the railroad from Madison to Indianapolis in the small community of Lancaster. Lancaster, often referred to as the "New England Settlement" was founded by a number of families from Vermont and Maine who were opposed to slavery. The college had an endowment of $100,000, which would be "appropriated to the education of the worthy and promising poor of both sexes, and of all complexions, preference being given to the colored so long as civil disabilities shall rest upon them" (Eleutherian College Exhibit).

Many of the trustees of the college also organized the Neil's Creek Anti-Slavery Society in 1839 and founded the Anti-Slavery Baptist Church in

Eleutherian College, outside of Madison, was created to offer education to both black and white students. It was founded by members of the Neil's Creek Anti-Slavery Society. *Author's collection.*

1846. Residents included Robert Elliot, John and Sarah Tibbets and Lyman and Aseneth Hoyt, all of whom became conductors on the UGRR.

Under the leadership of Thomas Cravens, the Lancaster group built Eleutherian College in 1856. By 1860, two hundred students attended the integrated institution, including fifty blacks from as far away as Mississippi and Louisiana. The college closed in 1937 but is now a historic landmark and is being restored as an educational museum center.

SHERIFF AND SLAVE CATCHER: ROBERT RIGHT REA (1800–1869)

The son of a Revolutionary War colonel, Robert Right Rea was the sheriff in Madison and was known for successfully catching fugitives and collecting and sharing bounty received for their capture. He is described as an enigma in many instances because he seemed personable and often associated with both slave capture and slave escapes. For instance, Robert Elliott, who lived ten miles north of Madison was a known UGRR conductor. Elliot's wife was a cousin of Sheriff Rea.

The John Todd house in Madison, built in 1830, had a special chimney constructed for the purpose of concealing slaves. "Reportedly, Todd and Rea conspired to hold the fugitives to see if a reward were offered for their return; if so, they would turn them over to their slaveholder's and collect the reward money. If there was no reward, the slaves would be taken through the Clifty Falls gorge up to Ryker's Ridge or the Michigan Road."[54]

Sheriff Rea owned livery stables near the Georgetown District in Madison. UGRR conductor George DeBaptiste stated in an interview that he "borrowed" horses during the night from the Rea stables to aid freedom seekers, sometimes "shodding" the horses' hooves with carpet to muffle the sound.[55]

When conductor Calvin Fairbanks was released from the Kentucky penitentiary in 1849, after serving his first term of imprisonment for aiding the Hayden family to freedom, he noted his first place of refuge: "On the 24th I left for Madison, Indiana, where I obtained lodgings with Wright Ray [sic], the famous slavehunter of that section. It was the first comfortable night's rest for near five years."[56]

Rea is known for many famous captures, including the White family case, involving Underground Railroad conductor Laura Haviland. The case involves the escape of the White family from Petersburg, Kentucky, to Rising

These buildings (close to the Georgetown District) were once stables owned by Sheriff Right Rea who was involved in many captures of fugitive slaves. *Author's collection*.

Sun, Indiana, with Rea capturing John White and taking him to Trimble County, Kentucky, close to a jail in Milton. By taking White to a Kentucky jail, it made it easier for Rea to dispose of White for sale or trade. Rea also captured Delia Webster when she was hiding from Newton Craig, warden at the Kentucky penitentiary, in Madison (see section under Delia Webster).

VEVAY, INDIANA

Vevay was established in 1814 as the county seat of Switzerland County. It began with the arrival of Swiss immigrants who started cultivating grapes for wineries and soon became a trading center and busy river port with grains, soybeans, tobacco and livestock becoming the mainstays of the county's agriculture. Ulysses Schenck was a riverboat captain and Swiss immigrant raised in Louisville who relocated to Vevay. He became known as the "Hay King" by exporting tons of hay with his fleet of flatboats and steamboats. He soon invested in other enterprises and became one of the wealthiest men in the area. The original Schenck house overlooks the river.

The Schenck Mansion Bed and Breakfast was built by his son, Benjamin Schenck, after the Civil War and is a thirty-five-room mansion that sits on a hillside overlooking Vevay.

As early as 1814, ferry service connected Indiana and Kentucky. At one time, there were seven ferry franchises along the Switzerland County shoreline, connecting to Kentucky towns such as Carrollton, Warsaw and Ghent. With its proximity to Kentucky, this active port would have been a place where hire outs of slaves would have taken place, much like other riverports on the free side of the river.

Hunter's Bottom in Trimble County, Kentucky, and the Fugitive Slave Act of 1850

Hunter's Bottom is a seven-mile stretch of road by the river on Highway 36. It is composed of fertile bottomlands, with steep hills to the south from Milton in Trimble County to Lost Creek in Carroll County. Beautiful antebellum homes lined this stretch of river with families prospering from the commerce generated in the area leading up to the Civil War. There are many homes that are still intact and well preserved, one of which is now the Richwood Bed and Breakfast.

The Richwood home was originally built by Samuel Fearn Jr. Samuel Fearn (1766–1828) brought his family to Hunter's Bottom and owned one thousand acres. His two sons, George and Samuel Jr., operated a large gristmill and a timber business and held other investments. Richard Daly, a slave on the Samuel Fearn Jr. farm, was a conductor on the UGRR and ferried many fugitives to Madison. Daly lived in a brick home behind Fearn's house. Daly's wife, Kitty, and four children were enslaved nearby by Mrs. Hoagland. When there was a chance that the family would be separated after Daly's wife died, he escaped with his children and settled in Windsor, Canada.[57]

A house in Hunter's Bottom that no longer stands is the Giltner Conway house. The Giltners initiated a court case that influenced the passage of the Fugitive Slave Act of 1850. Francis Giltner moved his family and slaves to the area in 1830 from Bourbon County, Kentucky. Adam Crosswhite and his family were enslaved by Francis Giltner.

In 1843, when Crosswhite learned that Giltner was going to sell part of his family, he took his wife, Sarah, and their four children and sought help through the UGRR in Madison. The Crosswhites successfully escaped and settled in Marshall, Michigan. A year or so later, Giltner's nephew Francis Troutman, along with David Giltner and James Lee, went to Marshall to retrieve the Crosswhites and bring them back to Kentucky. They were accompanied by the local deputy sheriff, Dixon, to the Crosswhite cabin. Adam and his son Johnson fled, but Troutman remained at the Crosswhite cabin with Adam's wife and other children while Giltner and Dixon went to secure a warrant. Neighbors came to the Crosswhites' rescue and protected the family from going back to Kentucky. While waiting for Giltner and Dixon at the Crosswhite cabin, Troutman got into a dispute with one of the neighbors, Mr. Hackett, and assaulted him. When Dixon returned, he charged Troutman with assault and battery and housebreaking. The next day, while Troutman was in court to pay $100 in fees before Judge Hobart, the neighbors and friends of the Crosswhites helped the family escape and board a train to Detroit. George DeBaptiste, the former UGGR conductor at Madison, Indiana, greeted the Crosswhites and took them to Canada.

As word about this incident spread across the country, it created a sensational reaction. Slave owners were furious that the townspeople in Michigan aided the Crosswhite family, and northerners in Michigan were equally outraged that a Kentucky posse tried to seize fugitives in a free state. Francis Troutman, who was also an attorney, represented the Giltners and returned to Michigan in 1848 and pressed charges against those who aided the Crosswhites. Justice McLane heard the *Giltner vs. Gorham* case in federal court, with the outcome awarding Giltner nearly $4,500 in damages and court costs.

During this time, momentum was gaining from Kentucky to pass legislature that would make it mandatory for U.S. marshals to seize runaway slaves in free states, with severe fines being placed on those harboring and aiding fugitives. The proposal went to the U.S. Senate and was led by Kentucky's Henry Clay (and close friend of Francis Giltner). It resulted in the Fugitive Slave Act of 1850.

The Fugitive Slave Act of 1850 was a game changer for fugitive slaves living in free soil. The 1850 act required that all escaped slaves, upon capture, be returned to their masters and that official and citizens of free stated had to cooperate. Many fugitives began to flee to Canada, which was outside the boundary of the law. It also increased the danger of living along the Ohio River for free blacks who were the subject of threats and intimidation tactics from slaveholders and bounty hunters who, without authority, searched their homes and trespassed on their property, supposedly searching for fugitives. On another note, it exposed those living in free states to a more visible and personal experience of slavery by witnessing families dragged, separated and forced back into slave labor by bounty hunters. Fortunately, other freedom seekers had been working on ways to help these refugees, and one of those was Henry Bibb.

Henry Bibb (1815–1854)

Henry Bibb's dream of freedom from enslavement began when he was a very young man. He was the son of Mildred Jackson, a slave, and James Bibb, but he never met his father. Bibb was born in Henry County and spent his early years in Trimble and Oldham Counties. He had six brothers, and they were separated and sold away. Bibb was hired out as a little boy, and his wages paid for the education of Harriet White, his playmate and owner. He learned to read and write through Harriet when she was having her lessons, noting later in his autobiography, "White children of slaveholders often taught slaves how to read and write."[58]

Henry married another slave, Malinda, and they had a daughter, Mary Frances. At that time, William Gatewood was their slaveholder, and they lived at the Gatewood Plantation outside of Bedford, about twelve miles from the Ohio River and Madison, Indiana. In 1837, with the permission of William Gatewood, Bibb went to Madison to earn wages by working in a slaughterhouse, but instead he took a steamboat to Cincinnati. From that moment, he began meeting people connected with the UGRR through Job Dundy, who told him about abolitionists who aided fugitives to escape to Canada. Bibb spent the winter in Perrysburg, Ohio, earning money to help him return to Kentucky to rescue his wife and daughter. He was captured by a "hostile mob" in his rescue attempt. The mob robbed him of his certificate from the Bedford Methodist Episcopal Church, the same church William Gatewood and former slaveholders, John and Alfred Sibley, attended. Gatewood sold Bibb and his family to slave trader Mathew Garrison in Louisville, and Garrison shipped them to the slave markets in New Orleans. Bibb and his family were bought by Deacon Whitfield from Claiborne Parrish, Louisiana.

Through a series of brutal treatment from Whitfield after an unsuccessful escape, Bibb was separated from his wife and daughter and never saw them again. He escaped to Detroit, and in October 1843, he attended the Michigan Convention of Colored Citizens. Soon, Bibb was recognized as a formidable speaker for the abolitionist cause.

Henry Bibb is featured for his sacrifices and contributions to end slavery in this exhibit at the Oldham County History Center. *Author's collection.*

Bibb gave his first lecture in May 1844, at the home of Laura Haviland, who was the founding member of the first antislavery society in Michigan. Haviland was an agent for the UGRR, and she also founded the Raisin Institute, a manual training school that included black students. Haviland also served as a teacher for Bibb when he organized the Refugee Home Society. Haviland is discussed in the next chapter regarding some cases in the Cincinnati area. Haviland made trips to Cincinnati and worked with Levi and Catherine Coffin to help plan slave escapes from Kentucky.

Bibb became an official antislavery lecturer, often presented along with Frederick Douglass, as a guest speaker for many rallies, conventions and occasions. Well-known newspaper owner and editor William Garrison ranked Henry Bibb, Wells Brown and Frederick Douglass as "the ablest speakers in the movement, the best qualified to address the public on the subject of slavery."[59]

In 1849, Henry Bibb published his narrative, *The Life and Adventures of Henry Bibb: An American Slave*, with support from the American and Foreign and Anti-Slavery Society. Money earned from his lectures and his narrative was used to purchase land for slave refugees near Windsor, Canada. He began publishing his abolitionist newspaper *Voice of a Fugitive*, which continued until his death in 1854. Bibb became close friends with George DeBaptiste. When George moved to Detroit in 1846, which was about the same time Bibb arrived. DeBaptiste purchased a steamboat to carry fugitives from Detroit to Amherstburg, Ontario, close to Bibb's fugitive colony.

Arrivals of fugitive slaves in Canada were frequently mentioned in *Voice of the Fugitive*, published semimonthly in Sandwich, Ontario, by Henry Bibb. In the issue on November 5, it boasted, "We can run a lot of slaves through from almost any of the bordering slave states into Canada within 48 houses and we defy the slaveholders and their abettors to beat that if they can."

On April 22, 1852, Bibb reported the arrival of fifteen slaves "within the last few days" and noted that "the Underground Railroad is doing good business this spring" and "especially the express train, is doing a good business just now. We have good and competent conductors—the road is doing better business this fall than usual."

No doubt Bibb was especially overjoyed when news came that some of his fellow slaves and old friends were arriving from his native state. "We are happy to announce the arrival of eight females by the last train of the Underground Railroad from Kentucky.…They are all one family consisting of a mother and her daughters…and it has scarcely ever been our lot to witness such a respectable and intelligent family of females from slavery… they will be an ornament in the future to our social circle in Canada."[60]

Bibb chaired the North American Convention of Colored People in 1851. He also founded the Anti-Slavery Society of Canada that same year. He was close friends with Josiah Henson (1789–1883) and together they formed the Fugitive Union Society in Canada to enable fugitives to "become owners and tillers of the soil."[61]

Bibb died of unknown causes as a young man of thirty-nine years. His second wife, Mary Miles, shared some of the success of the refugee colony and newspaper that was established in Canada. She became a well-known teacher and businesswoman and continued to support reform causes."[62] She lived for another twenty-three years after Bibb's death, and they have both been recognized as citizens of Canada.

Bibb died on August 1, which was known as Liberation Day, an international celebration recognizing August 1, 1833, when Great Britain liberated its slaves. Bibb had become an organizer for this annual celebration in Ontario. American blacks "drew inspiration from the day and hoped that the more than 3,000,000 of their enslaved kith and kin would one day, like their British empire cousins, break their chains and let freedom fly."[63] The Liberation Day activities had already been planned, and as news of

Bibb's death spread, the celebration took on even a greater meaning for the celebration of the life of a man who had given so much. George DeBaptiste was one of those in attendance.

Henry Bibb escaped six times and served eight masters. He was separated from his first wife and only child through slavery. He never got to see the reality of his dream for freedom in his native country.

Delia Webster

Delia Webster was a conductor for the UGRR and risked her life many times in freedom's cause. A native of Vergennes, Vermont, Webster was a teacher and had attended Oberlin College in Ohio (a well-known center of abolitionist and UGRR activity). From Oberlin, Webster procured a teaching job at the Lexington Female Academy in Lexington, Kentucky, "whose school received the patronage of the highest and wealthiest in the city."[64]

In her first venture with another conductor, Calvin Fairbank, they rescued Lewis Hayden and his family from Lexington, taking them to a crossing of the Ohio River at Maysville, Kentucky. On their return, both Webster and Fairbank were arrested and thrown in prison. Webster was the first woman that served time in a Kentucky penitentiary. Webster entered the Kentucky State Penitentiary in Frankfort on January 10, 1845, and received a pardon on Feburary 25, 1845. As the first woman jailed in the state prison, she had received an outpouring of public sympathy for her dismissal. Her partner, Calvin Fairbank, ended up serving four years, ten months and twenty-four days before receiving his pardon on August 23, 1849.[65]

In 1845, Webster purchased a six-hundred-acre farm in Trimble County with some partners. Almost directly across from Madison, Indiana, Trimble County was a prominent route for the UGRR. Soon slaves in the area began to disappear, and local slave owners grew incensed about Webster's well-known UGRR activities. On February 6, 1854, the community of Bedford drafted the following resolution: "Whereas it is known that Delia Webster had recently run off numerous slaves from Trimble County, therefore it is the will and determination of the citizens of said county that Miss Delia Webster leave the state."

The next day, about fifty slave owners rode to Webster's farm to make their demands and read the resolution. She turned on the crowd and admonished them for their cowardice of acting as a mob. The group left, somewhat with

UGGR conductor Delia Webster is portrayed by Erika Wardlow as a part of the educational programs at the Oldham County History Center. *Author's collection.*

their tails tucked between their legs. A month later, the mob reappeared at Webster's front door, threatening to burn down her home and dwellings, destroy her crops and livestock and assassinate her if she did not leave.

Six days later, the sheriff and his band returned to her house and arrested her. She spent some miserable weeks during a very cold snap in late winter and early spring in the primitive jailhouse in Beford. A few months later, she was to be indicted again, but she escaped across the river to Madison.

Newton Craig, Webster's jailor at the Kentucky penitentiary, sought her out for prosecution. Sheriff Rea in Madison captured Delia and put her in the Madison jail, and a hearing was set to determine whether it was legal for Webster to be sent back to Kentucky. It was determined that Webster would not be returned to Kentucky, which was met with cheers and support from locals who had attended the trial. However, Newton Craig, who had been staying in Madison during the trial was not so popular and was encouraged to leave town immediately. As Craig was waiting for the steamboat at the Madison docks, amid a somewhat hostel crowd, he was shot in the back. The shot was fired by Wendell Randall, who had been a tenant on the Webster farm. Randall received a three-year prison sentence in Indiana, and Craig survived the incident.[66]

Although now something of a refugee from Kentucky, Delia continued to operate her farm in Trimble County until 1868, when it was sold. She eventually moved to Iowa and died at the home of her niece in 1904. It is interesting to note that not far from the Webster Farm was the Preston Plantation. It was one of the largest plantations along the river. Owned by Mary Preston, it produced peaches and tobacco, among other commodities. Mary's father, Robert Wickliffe Sr., was among the slave owners with the most slaves in Kentucky. Mary and Delia Webster had met each other when Delia lived in Lexington. Oral tradition has it that Mary worked with Delia Webster on the UGRR and used the Preston plantation's river landings for sites of fugitive crossings into Indiana.[67]

WESTPORT, OLDHAM COUNTY, KENTUCKY

When Oldham County was created in 1824, it was carved out of land from Jefferson, Henry and Shelby Counties. The first courthouse was selected at Westport, a busy riverport with taverns, hotels, distilleries, tobacco warehouses and churches. The courthouse was constructed and in operation by 1828 and then moved to its more permanent location in LaGrange in 1838.

These early numbers of case records at Westport show how slavery influenced the day-to-day operation of the county. For instance it was ordered in March 1824 "that William Trigg, Captain John Abbott, Thomas Noel, Harrison Bright, James Trigg and Thomas Davidson be and they are hereby appointed patrollers in this county in the bounds of Captain Snowden's company of militia."[68] These patrollers would have been involved in runaway slave captures, and as such, they would be rewarded in bounty by the slaveholders.

Other appointments of the court included justice of the peace, tariff collectors on warehouses and road inspectors. All the appointees would earn income through these appointments. Henry Bibb's slaveholder, William Gatewood, appeared often at the Westport Courthouse and received appointments. In a list of allowances during the May term of the Oldham County Court in 1826, Gatewood received $59.50 for taking lists of taxable properties from landowners, which would have included slave lists. Slaves, like horses and other livestock, were taxable. Gatewood was indicted in the February term of 1831 for allowing his slave Mahala to hire herself out.

Mahala, thought to be Henry Bibb's wife's mother, was allowed "to go at large and hire herself out and trade at large contrary to the statute in such case made." It was OK to have hire out agreements made by slaveholders and those who wanted to lease a slave, but it was never okay for a slave to hire out themselves, although it was a very common practice. In fact, Gatewood allowed Henry Bibb to hire out himself when he went to Madison to look for work at the slaughterhouse, which became Bibb's first escape attempt from Kentucky.

The first murder case at the Oldham County court was a case of resistance to Lucy, who was enslaved by Elizabeth Smith. Lucy was indicted on May 18, 1825, for poisoning Elizabeth Smith by adding pulverized glass to a stew. It took Smith three days to die. Court records indicated that Lucy was indicted for murder and sentenced accordingly (in those years it would have been death by hanging). There are no records yet found of her execution.

In 1838, the Oldham County Courthouse moved from Westport, on the river, to its present site in LaGrange. In 1836, Trimble County was carved out of Henry and Oldham Counties, which skewed the votes to move the courthouse. The following stories took place at the Oldham County Courthouse in LaGrange.

JAMES MOUNT, OLDHAM COUNTY JAILOR, AND HIS WIFE, AMANDA RAILEY MOUNT

In 2018, we placed a Kentucky Historical Marker at the J.C. Barnett Library and Archives at the Oldham County History Center. This building was originally the home of James and Amanda Mount. In 2016, the site was designated as a site on the National Underground Railroad Network of the National Park Service because of a collection of family papers and artifacts that was donated by the Mount descendants.

In 2004, Lucretia Davenport donated this collection of artifacts that belonged to her late husband, John McRoberts Mount Jr. Mr. Mount inherited Grandma Railey's Box, a collection of letters and documents from his great-grandparents, James and Amanda Railey Mount. James and Amanda had two sons, John Jr. and Joseph Railey Mount. They were also appointed as wards to James's nephew, Amos Mount. Amanda Mount's great-grandmother was Elizabeth Randolph, sister to Jane, who was the mother of Thomas Jefferson.

The James and Amanda Mount house is now the J.C. Barnett Library and Archives at the Oldham County History Center. The Mounts were slave holders, and James served as the local jailer. Their family papers provide insight on slave holdings and activities on a local level. *Author's collection.*

In Grandma Railey's box there were thirty-two letters written by Amos to his aunt Amanda from his time fighting for the Union. Amos was seriously injured at Woodbury, near Murfreesboro, Tennessee, in 1863, but he survived, recovered and returned home to his beloved aunt Amanda. Later, he married and moved to Illinois.

There were also many receipts, bills of sales and slave documents. Like many other people in antebellum Kentucky with the means, the Mounts bought and sold slaves throughout the nineteenth century. As early as 1843, there is a bill of sale that indicates that James Mount purchased two slaves by the name Jeremiah and Lucy Jane for $500. In April 1846, a receipt shows that James Mount purchased a slave named William for $396 from William D. Mitchell, master in Chancery Court of Oldham County. A receipt dated April 12, 1848, from James Mount to J.J. Railey (brother of Amanda Railey Mount) details the payment for slaves who were part of Joseph Railey's (father of Amanda Railey Mount) estate in the amount of $465. Later, a receipt dated November 22, 1859 shows that Amanda Railey Mount bought a slave named George for $1,200.[69] These documents not only indicate that the Mounts bought and owned slaves but also that slaves ran away from the James Mount House, where the J.C. Barnett Archives and Library currently resides.

When President Abraham Lincoln issued the Emancipation Proclamation in January 1863, all slaves in the Confederacy were legally free, but this did not apply to Kentucky because Kentucky had joined the Union. In 1864, Lincoln declared that any slave that enlisted in the Union army would be given freedom, as well as freedom for his family. A flood of Kentucky slaves rushed to enlist at Camp Taylor in Louisville, Kentucky. Two receipts in the James and Amanda Mount collection indicate a blatant disregard for the law, as Amanda Mount is documented to have paid slave catchers twice to retrieve slaves who had gone to Louisville. In the first of these, Amanda Railey Mount paid William S. Bennett fifteen dollars "for trouble, expense, and taking runaway Negro soldier" to Louisville from LaGrange. Another receipt from Amanda Mount to J.W. Cardwell and Company (a company that wrote out contracts to make claims on enlisted runaways) states Amanda's claim for two slaves.

In addition to being a slave owner, James Mount served on the LaGrange Board of Trustees for some time and worked on the Jail Oversight Commission. In ads placed in a September issue of the *Louisville Journal*, James Mount announced the capture of three runaways, who were being held in the Oldham County jail. Bounty Hunters from Harney, Hughes and Company wrote to James Mount on August 9, 1862, requesting payment for capturing slaves in the advertisement.

The Mount documents demonstrate how communities in slave states operated on the forced sale of runaway slaves. Courthouses in county government were sites of auctions and disposition of property, of which enslaved people were considered. Local jailors also housed runaway slaves and received payment for claimants. Public whippings and hangings took place on the courthouse lawns. Slaves were listed as property in the tax laws as well, so the county collected money from slaveholders who listed the numbers of slaves on their annual property taxes. Lastly, local sheriffs and justices of the peace worked with bounty hunters and appointed patrols to capture runaway slaves.

REVEREND BARTLETT TAYLOR BUYS HIS FREEDOM AT THE OLDHAM COUNTY COURTHOUSE DOOR

Bartlett Taylor was enslaved by the Jonathan Taylor family and grew up on their farm six miles north of LaGrange. At nineteen, he was sold to Mr.

The Oldham County Courthouse (circa 1875) replaced the courthouse built here in 1828, which was the site, like almost all rural courts in Kentucky, of slave auctions and other slave-related court cases. *Author's collection.*

Berry and became a hire-out in Louisville, where he learned to be a butcher under Mr. Clisindoff. He saved $1,800 and fell in love and wanted to get married but not until he was a free man. He lent his money to some friends in need, but he also wrote to his owner, Mr. Berry, expressing his wish to buy his freedom.

On September 20, 1840, he went to the Oldham County Courthouse and was put on the auction block. He was sold for $2,000, himself being the highest bidder. Mr. Brent, the agent for the sale, let Taylor make a promissory note for the $2,000, and Taylor, true to his promise, paid him back promptly. Taylor married Mrs. Jane McCune of Abington, Virginia, as a free man.

Mr. Taylor became a prominent citizen in Louisville, establishing a beef business and accumulating money and real estate. His wife died, and he remarried Miriam McGill. He had three daughters and one son. He became a founder of many churches throughout Kentucky and served as a missionary in both Kentucky and Tennessee.[70]

HERMITAGE FARM

Hermitage Farm is perhaps the most well-known farm in Oldham County and is now a tourism site for several reasons. The farm was established in 1830 by the Henshaw family, in whose possesion it remained until it was sold in 1936 to Warner Jones. Jones developed the farm for Thoroughbred race horses, which sired national winners such as the 1953 Kentucky Derby Winner, Dark Star.

Hermitage was created from the purchase of surveyed land in the late 1700s by Captain John Henshaw in Virginia. The land passed from to his son, John Henshaw, who gave one thousand acres each to his sons, Phillip Telfair Henshaw and John Henshaw. Hermitage Farm was created by Phillip out of his portion of land. Philip and his wife, Sarah Ann Scott Henshaw, moved to Oldham County and began the construction of the Hermitage house, which was completed in 1835.

The 1830 census for Philip Henshaw shows fifty people living at the farm—forty-three of whom were enslaved. The 1850 slave schedule for Sarah Ann Scott Henshaw shows thirty-two slaves on the farm.[71]

During the construction of Hermitage, the Henshaws returned to Virginia for a visit, and Phillip got typhoid fever and died. Sarah Ann Henshaw returned to Hermitage with their three small children, Sarah Ann Elizabeth, John Scott and Lucy Mary Jane. Lucy Mary Jane married Richard Waters in the mid-1800s. Also living at the farm at that time was Sarah Ann Scott Henshaw, who lived there until her death in 1862.

The Waters had five children, one of whom, Phillip Edmund Waters, was given the farm. Phillip introduced orchard grass to the area, and it eventually became a major crop for farmers in the area, making Oldham County the orchard grass capital of the world.

The Hermitage House is in the typical style of Kentucky planters who came to the frontier and began clearing land and setting up estates modeled after their Virginia plantations. Most of these planters were children and grandchildren of Revolutionary War parents—privileged "landed gentry" from Virginia, Maryland and Pennsylvania building large brick mansions with outbuildings and slave quarters, raising crops and livestock. These larger estates in Kentucky included John Speed's Farmington, William Bullitt's Oxmoor plantation, Robert Wickliffe's Glendower, Henry Clay's Ashland and General Levi Todd's Ellerslie, many of which had more than forty or fifty slaves on their property lists.

In the Oldham County area there was a large number of Taylors, all descended from the union of Martha Thompson to John Taylor II in 1699. This included Commodore Richard Taylor and two U.S. presidents, Zachary Taylor and James Madison. The largest slaveholders in Arkansas were a Taylor couple, John Martin and Elizabeth Rives Taylor, who also had a farm in Oldham County.

JOHN MARTIN AND ELIZABETH RIVES TAYLOR: KENTUCKY COTTON PLANTERS AND SLAVEHOLDERS

The Taylor family split their lives each year living in both Kentucky and Arkansas, using the Ohio River as their transportation between homes. They operated a ten-thousand-acre cotton planation by Bayou Bartholomew near the Mississippi River and a three-hundred-acre tobacco and livestock farm at Westport in Oldham County, Kentucky.

Mauvilla was a palatial, eighteen-room brick mansion in Westport that was built by Dr. John Martin Taylor (1819–1884) and his wife, Mary Elizabeth Robertson Rives Taylor (1824–1868). John Martin Taylor was a cousin of Zachary Taylor. Their large dogtrot log home called Hollywood was on the ten-thousand-acre cotton plantation.

The Taylors used slaves for their cotton operation in Arkansas and their farm operation in Kentucky. The 1860 census records of slave schedules for John Martin Taylor from Drew and Desha Counties in Arkansas indicate listings for 184 slaves. This made them the largest slaveholders in Arkansas. In Oldham County, a tax census from the same period shows that the Taylors listed a total of 23 slaves, with only 8 older than sixteen, with a total value of $8,050.

The University of Arkansas has restored the Hollywood home and conducted archaeological studies at that site. Down the road from the Taylor house were the slave quarters with a church and graveyard. There is a small Taylor graveyard at Hollywood where John Martin is buried. His wife, Elizabeth, died at the Mauvilla house from complications during childbirth, and she is buried at the Cave Hill Cemetery in Louisville. When in Kentucky, two of their sons attended the Kentucky Masonic College in LaGrange. In all, the Taylors had ten children, seven of whom made it to adulthood.

When the Civil War was near its end, John Taylor told slaves in Arkansas that they would be transported back to Kentucky if they wanted. Elizabeth Martin accompanied the slaves by steamboat, with a transfer at Cairo,

Mauvilla was built by John and Elizabeth Taylor near Westport. They also owned a ten-thousand-acre cotton plantation, Hollywood, at the Bayou Bartholomew in Arkansas. They owned the most slaves in Arkansas and traveled between their two estates several times during the year. *Oldham County Historical Society.*

Illinois. People in Cairo were furious at the sight of the slave mistress with her slaves and began to riot. A Union officer, Captain Kiteby, intervened and escorted Taylor and the slaves on the boat to Westport.[72]

Mauvilla was torn down in the 1950s, but was one mile from Westport on Highway 524, along the Ohio River. The house had a long avenue that led from the house, which sat on a rise directly to the river with a landing. The restored Hollywood home in Arkansas is the only known extant dogtrot home from that time period in Arkansas.

SCENIC BYWAYS

Kentucky Side

A fifteen-mile section of US Highway 42 is a designated scenic byway in Oldham County and includes historic Hermitage and Ashbourne Farms, which are now event centers.

County Road Highway 524 runs in a semicircle off US Highway 42 in Oldham County, partly along Ohio River, and includes Westport, a river town, slave auction site and home to the John Martin Taylor and Elizabeth Rives house.

Highway 36 from Milton to Carrollton, including Hunter's Bottom, is the site of many antebellum homes, two of which, the Fearn Plantation and Giltner Plantation (no longer extant), had well-known, documented cases.

Indiana Side

Ohio River Scenic Byway, State Route 56 runs from Madison to Vevay. Vevay was a large shipping port during the 1800s.

PLACES TO VISIT

KENTUCKY SIDE

The Oldham County History Center

The Oldham County History Center offers two National Park Service Passport Stamps: The Bibb Escapes/Gatewood plantation and the James and Amanda Mount home. Both are part of the National Park Service National Underground Railroad Network. The campus has recently undergone a $2 million renovation and includes four nineteenth-century buildings: The Peyton Samuel Head Family Museum (circa 1840), the J.C. Barnett Library and Archives (James and Amanda Mount House, circa 1840), the Root Cellar (circa 1840) and the Rob Morris Chapel Education Building (circa 1880), along with a recently added Dahlgren Barn that features a hand-built colonial fireplace and bread oven.

The hands-on, interactive museum focuses on life in the nineteenth and twentieth centuries in Oldham County. Exhibits include slavery (Henry Bibb, Delia Webster and Richard James Oglesby), the Ohio River, Pewee Valley and the Little Colonel book series, D.W. Griffith Movie Theatre, World War II oral histories, Hermitage and Ashbourne Farms and the Kentucky State Penitentiary. Programs are offered throughout the year, and walking tours are available.

Website: www.oldhamcountyhistoricalsociety.org
Address: 106 North Second Avenue, LaGrange, Kentucky
Phone: (502) 222-0826

The Oldham County History Center in LaGrange features four restored nineteenth-century buildings and has an extensive collection of court documents and family papers. The center holds two designations on the National Park Service National Underground Railroad Network. *Author's collection.*

Northwestern Colored Cemetery: Historic African American Cemeter, LaGrange, Kentucky

This cemetery was formally established in 1889 as the Northwestern Colored Cemetery Company by trustees John Taylor, John "Bullitt" Washington and John Vancleve. The older graves date to shortly after the Civil War, with possibly some pre–Civil War burials. The grave of Petter Parker lists his slave history, which is very unusual. There are several burials of Civil War soldiers (Rufus Holt and Alex Beaumont) and World War I Buffalo Soldiers. Washington Bullitt, a friend of abolitionist Elijah Marrs who helped establish education classes in the local black churches, is buried here. Some of the gravestones were handmade by local resident Tommy Lee during the early and mid-twentieth century. The Oldham County History Center has maps and more information. The cemetery is located at the end of Third Street where it intersects with Fourth Street.

Hermitage Farm

The farm remained in family hands until it was bought by Warner and Harriet Jones in 1936. The Joneses began a Thoroughbred horse operation, producing Derby winner Dark Star in 1953. The queen of England visited Hermitage in 1986 to look over the Thoroughbred stock. Warner Jones is still the only person to breed winners of the Kentucky Derby (Dark Star), the Kentucky Oaks (Nancy, Jr.) and the Breeder's Cup (Is It True). Warner Jones died in 1994. The farm is now in conservation easement and is a tourism site. There is a restaurant and bourbon bar (opening early 2020) with future plans for a local farmer's market. The farm offers Thoroughbred horse tours, accomodations and event rentals.

Website: http://hermitagefarm.com
Address: 10500 West Highway 42, Prospect, Kentucky
Phone: (502) 228-1426

Westport in Oldham County

This small river port was settled in the late 1700s by one of its first business operators Levi Bowyer, who had a tavern and supply house on the Indiana side. Pioneers could unload their flatboats and journey up the road from Bowyer's to the Northwest Territory. The first courthouse (circa 1828) for Oldham County is now occupied by the Westport Methodist Church.

The Northwestern Colored Cemetery in LaGrange has burials from before the Civil War and the graves of notable civil rights leaders such as Washington Bullitt. *Author's collection.*

Hermitage Farm was established by the Henshaw family in 1828. The slaveholding family came from Virginia and established an orchard grass crop, which established Oldham County as the orchard grass capital through most of the twentieth century. The farm exchanged ownership in 1936 to Warner and Harriet Jones and quickly rose to the top as a Thoroughbred horse farm. Hermitage is now a tourism site with various activities, including a bourbon bar and restaurant. *Author's collection.*

The first courthouse (circa 1828) for Oldham County is now occupied by the Westport Methodist Church. There is a historical marker at the courthouse where William Gatewood, slaveholder of Henry Bibb, was involved in court cases and warrants. *Author's collection*.

There is a historical marker at the courthouse where William Gatewood, slaveholder of Henry Bibb, was involved in court cases and warrants. Westport is also a journal entry in Alexis de Toqueville's *Democracy in America*. His party had to depart its boat here because the Ohio River was frozen. The group continued its journey to Louisville on horseback. There is a marker at the community square by the Westport Methodist Church that commemorates Toqueville's journey. Westport has a nice view of the river with a small park, restrooms, a play and picnic area and a public boat ramp.

Bedford Courthouse Square in Trimble County

Henry Bibb, Delia Webster and Elijah Anderson all served time at the Bedford jail. The current stone jail was built in the 1880s on the site of the original structure. The earlier jail was probably a two-story log building. There is a historical marker for Delia on the courthouse lawn. Two blocks north of the courthouse is a privately owned white church, which was the Methodist Church that Henry Bibb was allowed to attend. The Sibley

The Bedford jail, built in the 1880s, resides on the original site of the jail that housed UGGR conductors Delia Webster, Elijah Anderson and Henry Bibb. *Author's collection.*

families and Gatewood family also attended this church and allowed Bibb to hold a membership card. The courthouse is located in the center of this small town on Highway 42

Little Kentucky River Winery

The Little Kentucky River Winery follows the ridgeline of the Little Kentucky River where the Sibley family lived. The Sibleys, as slaveholders, split up Henry Bibb's family when Albert Sibley moved to Missouri and took two of Henry's brothers with him.

Local wineries have made a comeback in Kentucky, which was the home of the first commercial winery in the United States, started by Marquis de Lafayette's winemaker, Jean-Jacques Dufour, in 1798 in Lexington. Slave labor operated the vineyard. In his discussion of starting a winery in Kentucky, Dufour suggested the following:

> *The produce of 160 shares to be appropriated as follows:*
>
> | | |
> |---|---|
> | *For 633 acres of land* | *$633* |
> | *For 5 families of negroes* | *$5,000* |
> | *For tools, vituals, and other support, until the place would be productive* | *$1000* |
> | *Expenses of getting vine scions,* | *$800* |
> | *Incidental expenses* | *$567* |
> | ***Total*** | ***$8000*** |

Little Kentucky River supports local history projects and has put history themes into its various offerings of wine. The farm includes an outdoor pavilion with Saturday tastings, music and food during the summer months. The other location is in the LaGrange Trackside Winery in the historic district of LaGrange, located along the railroad tracks of Main Street.

Website: www.thelittlekentuckyriverwinery.com
Farm address: 3289 Highway 421 South, Bedford, Kentucky
Trackside address: 205 East Main Street, LaGrange, Kentucky
Email: tweyler@gmail.com

Delia Webster Historical Markers in Trimble County

There are two markers that are a tribute to Delia Webster in Trimble County. Historical Marker no. 1099 at the junction of Route 1256 and Detmer Road was erected near the Webster Farm, which is under private ownership and runs down to the Ohio River. Historical marker no. 1822 at the Bedford courthouse mentions her stay at the Bedford jail, which was located at the site of the current stone jail built in the 1880s.

Hunter's Bottom

Hunter's Bottom in Milton is composed of seven miles of bottomland along the Ohio River, stretching from Milton in Trimble County to three miles west of Carrollton along State Road Highway 36. At least fifteen sites have

The Richwood Bed and Breakfast, was the original home of Samuel Fearn Jr. Fearn and his brother, George, were wealthy entrepreneurs and slaveholders. Richwood is an example of several antebellum estates along this section of road by the Ohio River known as Hunter's Bottom. *Author's collection.*

been identified here as constructed during antebellum Kentucky. Some of these sites have been restored, such as the Sam Fearn Jr. Richwood Plantation, which is now an event center and Giltner plantation (no longer extant), which had well-known, documented cases.

INDIANA SIDE

Madison

Madison Historic District, Jefferson County

Madison is a beautiful river town with well-preserved buildings within a large historic district. There are several house museums, restaurants and activities for families. The most important area here is the Georgetown District and the Jefferson County Courthouse. The courthouse was built in 1855 on the same site as the original, which was built in 1823 and was lost due to fire. The dome caught fire in 2009 but was restored. After another escape from the hands of a Trimble County posse, Delia resided in Madison

The Madison courthouse was the center of court activity for cases such as the Delia Webster trial. *Author's collection.*

for a short period. Her old jailer from Kentucky, Newton Craig, sought to bring her back to Kentucky for her aiding a fugitive. The courthouse marks the site where a hearing was held regarding the return of Delia Webster to Kentucky. The court ruled in favor of Webster. The courthouse is open to the public Monday through Friday from 8:00 a.m. until 4:00 p.m.

Address: 300 East Main Street, Madison, Indiana

Eleutherian College

Eleutherian was a word used in the 1840s and '50s and is defined as "a frantic zeal for freedom." The college was founded by a group of Baptists who formed the Neil's Creek Anti-Slavery Society in 1839 in the small town of Lancaster. This three-story limestone building accepted all students—black, white, male or female. The board of directors today is restoring the college and offers free public tours and various activities throughout the year.

Website: www.eleutherian-college.org
Address: 6927 Indiana State Road 250, Madison, Indiana
Phone: (812) 866-7129

Georgetown District

The Georgetown Neighborhood was composed of free blacks who settled in the area as early as 1820. The neighborhood included some prominent abolitionists and UGRR conductors, such as George DeBaptiste, William J. Anderson and Elijah Anderson. The area includes six blocks of homes, churches and businesses, which are a combination of Federal, Greek Revival and Italianate styles from the early to mid-1800s. It was the first district recognized in the National Underground Railroad Network to Freedom program. Check with the Jefferson County History Museum for a self-guided brochure or Historic Madison.

Website: www.historicmadisoninc.com
Address: 500 West Street, Madison, Indiana
Phone: (812) 265-2967

Jefferson County History Museum and Waterfront Park

The Jefferson County History Museum has a well-organized archive and library, as well as exhibits on local topics with hands-on activities. The museum sponsors programs and topics on the UGRR and works in partnership with Eleutherian College. There is also a separate facility that focuses on trains and train history. Historic walking tours begin here, and information on tours, including the Georgetown Historical Interpretive Walking Tour, can be found here. There is also a nice publication available: "Historic African-American Sites and Structures Jefferson County, Indiana," which was published by the African American Cultural Preservation project of the African American Landmarks committee. The museum is located near the Madison Waterfront Park, which features paved walkways and benches to view the Ohio River.

Website: www.jeffersonhistorycenter.org
Address: 615 West First Street, Madison, Indiana
Phone: (812) 265-2335

The Madison waterfront offers a paved walkway and views of the Ohio River. The Imus Overlook along the walk is directly across from the Delia Webster farm and crossing for fugitive slaves. *Author's collection.*

Clifty Falls State Park

Established in 1920, Clifty Falls State Park features a narrow valley, sheer cliffs and plunging waterfalls with a trail to an observation tower that overlooks the Ohio River Valley and town of Madison. Ryker's Ridge nearby was also a known crossing on the UGRR. There is an outdoor swimming pool, a nature center, the Clifty Falls Inn and ten walking trails with different levels of difficulty. Reservations for the inn and campground must be made online.

Campgrounds website: www.camp.IN.gov
Inn website: www.indianainns.com
Address: 1501 Green Road, Madison, Indiana
Phone: (812) 273-8885

Switzerland County

Vevay, Indiana

The town has a walking tour of all the historic buildings, and there is an aggressive tourism program, Switzerland County Tourism, that promotes activities and festivals. There are many places on the list of National Register of Historic Places (pre–Civil War) within both the town and Switzerland County. The Thiebaud Farmstead and Musée de Venoge, located outside of Vevay, provided demonstrations and lifestyle depictions that mimic antebellum lifestyle. Find more information at the Switzerland County Tourism Office located at the Phoenix Hotel.

Website: www.switzcotourism.com
Address: 120 West Main Street, Vevay, Indiana
Phone: (812) 427-3237

Vevay Museum and Church

The Switzerland County History Museum and the Life on the Ohio River Museum are a combination of two buildings. They highlight local culture and life from Native Americans to Swiss settlers and feature a diverse collection of life along the Ohio River, from the earliest flatboats to steam packets and towboats. According to researcher Diane Coon, the 1860 Greek Revival Presbyterian Church, which houses various local collections,

Clifty Falls State Park outside Madison provides a beautiful tower overlook of Madison and the Ohio River. This was also a busy area as a crossing on the UGRR. *Author's collection.*

The Ulysses Schenck mansion overlooks the Ohio River at Vevay. Ulysses invested heavily in flatboats and ship building and expanded his business to furniture-making and agriculture and became known as the Hay King because of the enormous quantity of hay he purchased and sold. His business efforts would have included associations with Kentucky slaveholding farms and operations. *Author's collection.*

The Life on the River Museum at Vevay includes exhibits and information on steamboats, wineries, early settlements in the area and associations with Kentucky agriculture. *Author's collection.*

was originally chartered in 1820 and was led by Reverend James Duncan and Judge Stephen C. Stevens, who were two radical antislavery members in those early years.[73]

Website: www.switzcomuseums.org
Address: 208 and 210 East Market Street, Vevay, Indiana
Phone: (812) 427-3560

4

A FREE METROPOLIS

Cincinnati and Northern Kentucky

Ohio's not the place for me;
For I was much surprised
So many of her sons to see
In garments of disguise
Her name has gone thro-out the world
Free Labour, Soil and Men
But slaves had better far be hurled
Into the Lion's Den.
So Farewell, Ohio!
I'm not safe in thee:
I'll travel on to Canada
Where colored men are free.
—From *Voice of the Fugitive* newspaper

Cincinnati grew into a thriving metropolis during the nineteenth century. With the completion of the Erie-Ohio Canal in 1845 and the expansion of railroad construction, Cincinnati could expand trade and business using the Ohio River and reach into the Great Lakes. Cincinnati became a supplier of many products, of which the chief export became pork, earning its nickname of Porkopolis. The city also became the largest manufacturer of steamboats, attracting all of the associated subsidiary businesses.

These opportunities attracted German and Irish immigrants in large numbers, and by the end of the Civil War, Germans composed 30 percent

Cincinnati wharf area along the river around the turn of the century. *87.70.43. A.W. Terhune Collection, Archives and Library Collection, University of Louisville.*

of the population. Black communities had settled into the Queen City and had become an early native population but were threatened and subjected to racist bias due to the proximity of the slave trade across the river in Covington. Blacks, for the most part, had little prospects for upward mobility in the workforce because of the lack of educational opportunities. As Irish immigrants moved into the region, they competed with blacks for labor-intensive and low-paying jobs, adding to another layer of prejudice and competition for black workers.

The mix of free blacks on the north shore of the Ohio River and enslaved blacks on the south shore threatened slaveholders who were increasingly edgy and fearful of losing their "property." Stories of resistance and slave uprisings, such as John Brown's Raid on Harpers Ferry and Nat Turner's Rebellion, along with narratives of successful slave escapes and abolitionist newspapers, gave encouragement and hope for other freedom seekers to cross the borderland.

Black Laws were created in these borderland "free" states to discourage black settlements and deny blacks equal rights. These laws were passed in part to reduce the influence of free blacks because of the potential they had to harbor and help fugitive slaves. Slave laborers provided the menial labor needed for iron foundries; hemp, corn and tobacco production;

manual construction; slaughterhouse work; and movement of goods and cargo on ships. Slave laborers worked on both sides of the river, under permission and control of the slaveholders. Free blacks, new immigrants and enslaved workers worked side by side. This mix of workers created a strange context of racial bias on many different levels as people were defining the American dream.

Cincinnati, in particular, was strict because of the concern of slaves entering the city and congregating on their days off. Slaveholders let their laborers cross the river, often at liberty, to work and to spend leisure time, and free blacks crossed over to the Kentucky side in Covington. On the Kentucky side, the City of Covington did not want free blacks wandering around their streets and passed ordinances to restrict the "loitering" of free blacks. Cincinnati passed ordinances to excluded blacks from benefits of the Poor Fund and excluded their admission to the infirmary, hospitals, poor houses and so on.[74] Blacks had to obtain assurances and secure bonds under the sponsorship of whites if they wanted to purchase property. Blacks were often cajoled and harassed by local sheriffs and bounty hunters who were in search of fugitives, particularly after the Fugitive Act of 1850.

The allure of a large "free" metropolis across the river from a slave state was too much to resist, in spite of Black Laws, harassment and threat of repudiation. Fugitives could blend in at the free black settlements in a big city. People like Henry Bibb had successfully traveled the route back and forth several times. Frederick Douglass, Lewis Hayden, Harriet Tubman, Sojourner Truth and Josiah Henson, among others, had broken the chain. Their stories were public, inspiring and invoked support. Cincinnati became the most popular and attractive route on the UGRR as abolitionists took root in the Queen City to help fugitives on their northward journeys.[75]

Slaves living in the vicinity of the Ohio River knew blacks residing on free soil and went to their homes seeking advice and assistance. A young Frankfort fugitive disappeared while on a trip with his mistress in Cincinnati. Police tracked him down to a woman who lived on Sixth Street in Bucktown in Cincinnati. The woman "raised a shout," and people began pouring into the streets, allowing the fugitive to escape in the crowd. John Hatfield, a free black, recalled how a slave catcher intercepted a group of Kentucky fugitives who were crossing the river and concealed them in a basement, waiting for the rest of his men. When area blacks realized what was happening, they sneaked the fugitives out of the basement two at a time, until all thirteen were free.[76]

THE LANE SEMINARY AND HARRIET BEECHER STOWE

The Lane Theological Seminary opened in 1833 in the Walnut Hills area of Cincinnati. The seminary was a Presbyterian outpost to train young men who were interested in theology. The first president of the school was Dr. Lyman Beecher (1775–1863). Beecher moved his family from Connecticut to Cincinnati. Beecher was a Yale graduate and was one of the cofounders of the American Temperance Society. The seminary was located just a few blocks from the Beecher house. He was also the pastor of the Second Presbyterian Church in Cincinnati. Harriet Beecher Stowe was one of Lyman Beecher's daughters.

Under the sponsorship and organization of Theodore Weld, a series of seminars was held at Lane on the topic of slavery. These Lane debates took place in 1833 and 1834, each lasting eighteen days. The debates pitted those advocating the colonization of slaves (sending former slaves back to Africa) against those in favor immediate emancipation. The debates received national attention. Local business leaders were outraged by the activities of the debates and forced the school to abandon future discussions on abolition. Slaveholders from Kentucky came in and incited mob violence. Beecher himself opposed the position of abolition and refused to offer classes to African American students. These debates were well attended and included attorney Salmon Chase and Harriet Beecher.

The students from these debates became passionate about abolition of slavery and, without the permission of the trustees of the seminary, formed a school to teach African Americans to read. The fifty-one students became known as the Lane Rebels and were dismissed by the seminary. Thirty-two of them left Cincinnati and went to Oberlin College.

The religious center in Ohio most known for the aid of refugees was the Congregational Colony and Oberlin College. When the Lane Rebels largely transferred from Lane Seminary to Oberlin in 1835, it became known as a hotbed of abolitionism. From 1835 to 1860, Oberlin was a busy station on the Underground Railroad, receiving passengers from at least five converging lines. Several of the conductors mentioned in this book went there, including Delia Webster, Calvin Fairbank, John G. Fee and James Author Thome.[77]

HARRIET BEECHER STOWE AND *UNCLE TOM'S CABIN*

Harriet Beecher Stowe (1811–1896) was the seventh of thirteen children of Lyman Beecher. Harriet's mother, Roxana, died when Harriet was only five. Harriet was educated in Connecticut at the Harford Female Seminary and moved to Cincinnati in 1832 to join her father when she was twenty-one. She was a member of a literary and social club in Cincinnati that included the young lawyer Salmon P. Chase. It was there that she also met her husband, Calvin Ellis Stowe, a widower who was a professor at Lane Seminary and an ardent abolitionist.

During her years in Cincinnati, Harriet visited both sides of the Ohio River and personally witnessed the stories and experiences of enslavement. When Harriet's cook, a former slave, explained how her slaveholder became the father of her children, Harriet was exposed to the sexual realities forced on slave women. When John Birney's office, which produced abolitionist newspaper the *Philanthropist*, was burned down by a mob of white Cincinnatians in 1836, Harriet composed an editorial in protest.

John Rankin, a well-known abolitionist and UGRR conductor in Ripley, Ohio, became an acquaintance of Harriet's through his son Adam, who attended Lane Seminary. Calvin Stowe was Adam's professor. The Stowes became active conductors for the UGRR. Adam Rankin even assisted Harriet in delivering fugitive slaves to Quaker William Butterworth, who lived twenty-five miles north of Cincinnati.[78]

Reverend John Rankin shared with Harriet his stories of enslavement and the fugitive slaves who he assisted in Ripley, Ohio, which was located fifty-three miles northeast of Cincinnati, along the Ohio River. The most famous of these was the Eliza Harris story. Eliza was an extremely brave woman whose courage and tenacity earned her a place in the annals of freedom seekers and defenders for democracy.

Eliza's story became the backdrop for Harriet's famous novel *Uncle Tom's Cabin*, published in 1852. Beecher created her characters from portraits of stories and places that she had heard about and visited. For example, her description of a slave auction was taken from her visit at the Marshall Key house in Washington, Kentucky. Colonel Marshall Key was the county clerk of Mason County Circuit Court and was a slaveholder. The courthouse, where slave auctions often took place, was located in proximity of his home. Beecher visited with Colonel Key's daughter, Elizabeth Marshall Key, a former pupil of Harriet's, at the Key home.[79] (Interesting to note that Elizabeth later married Thomas Henry Nelson, Abraham

Lincoln's ambassador to Chile and President Ulysses Grant's ambassador to Mexico).

Living in Cincinnati during the 1830s and '40s provided Harriet with unlimited access to stories and incidents about slavery, fugitive slaves, the UGRR and conductors who could impassion a talented author like Stowe. The model for her uncle Tom came through her friendships with people like Josiah Henson, a fugitive slave, writer, impassioned abolitionist speaker and new Canadian resident who later helped Henry Bibb establish support for Canadian refugees. When Harriet visited her brother Henry Ward Beecher in Indianapolis between 1840 and 1847, she frequently visited with Tom and Sarah Magruder, former slaves from a Kentucky family. The Magruder's six children, Tom, Sarah, Louisa, Moses, Peter and Topsy, are thought to have been inspiration for the fictious children in her novel with the same names.[80]

John Van Zandt, Calvin Fairbank and John Fairfield were models of renegade conductors who often risked life and limb to assist fugitives. They moved fugitives through the UGRR in Ripley, Cincinnati, Madison and Louisville. Calvin Fairbank spent a good portion of his adult life in Kentucky prisons for his activities to help fugitives escape.

Stowe became good friends with Quakers Levi and Catherine Coffin when they moved to Cincinnati from their home in Newport, Indiana, where they had conducted UGRR activities for twenty years. The Coffins began working with a group of Quakers that promoted the production and sale of goods only produced by free labor. In 1846, the Coffins moved to their new home, just a block away from the Stowe house on Gilbert Avenue, to manage the Free Produce Association, a wholesale mercantile business, which was a free trade concept. Keeping their Newport home open and operated by others as a refuge for the UGRR, the Coffin's also became prominent conductors in Cincinnati. Stowe's characters named Simeon and Rachel Halliday were based on the Coffins.

Stowe used Christianity throughout the novel as a powerful weapon that challenged proslavery southern Christian churches that used the Bible to sanctify the system of slavery. By using the tenements of duty, honor, faith and forgiveness as the base of Christian hope in resurrection, Stowe created her uncle Tom as a Christ figure who gave his life for the freedom of others. In the context of nineteenth-century America, this created a dilemma for any church that promoted enslavement with Christian authority. The American Missionary Society, AME Churches and other religious affiliations associated in the abolitionist movement gained tremendous support through the creation of Uncle Tom.

All of these people who passed through Stowe's life, many whom had experienced the borderland of the Ohio River, were pieces of the quilt that created her novel. *Uncle Tom's Cabin* became the best-selling novel in the nineteenth century, followed by the Bible. In the first year, it sold three hundred thousand copies in the United States; in Great Britain one million copies were sold. The novel reached into mainstream America and evoked sympathy for slaves for many people who were not aware or exposed to the frontline of this brutal system. Today the novel is criticized for stereotyping blacks into subservient role models that persisted through twentieth-century America. That case could be argued if it were not for the persistent racism that continued during the Reconstruction years and beyond, supported by centuries of racist culture fueled by the greed and profits of those who benefitted from the selling of human chattel.

LEVI (1798–1877) AND CATHERINE COFFIN (1803–1881)

Levi and Catherine Coffin were Quakers who moved to Newport, Indiana (now Fountain City), in 1826 and were involved in providing assistance to fugitive slaves, both by keeping them in their home and by providing assistance for their freedom and journey north. They were so prominent in their efforts that Levi Coffin became known as the Father of the Underground Railroad. After twenty years at their home in Newport, they moved to Cincinnati where "four branches of the Road" had developed as routes north to Canada for freedom seekers.[81] Businesses and Quaker groups encouraged the Coffins to set up a "free trade" business in Cincinnati that promoted the sale of goods made by free labor. Levi set up his warehouse at Sixth and Elm Streets.[82]

Catherine got involved in the Anti-Slavery Women's Sewing Society, which produced clothing for fugitives who often had little but the clothes on their backs. Catherine Coffin was an excellent seamstress and was known to construct outfits to disguise fugitives as they walked through the Cincinnati streets. Her favorite disguise was to make a Quaker outfit with a large bonnet that would hide a person's face.

In his book *Reminiscences of Levi Coffin*, Coffin provides some of the best firsthand accounts on the operation of the UGRR. The Coffins were very successful in raising money for the antislavery cause and, at times, helped to buy freedom for slaves through agents at auction sites. It is estimated that the Coffins assisted more than three thousand slaves during their lifetimes in

Newport and Cincinnati. After the Civil War, Levi Coffin continued to assist the newly freed slave population, raising more than $100,000 for the Western Freedmen's Aid Society in one year. When Levi Coffin died, hundreds gathered to mourn his loss. His pallbearers were free blacks who had assisted him with UGRR activities. He and Catherine, who died four years later, are buried at the Spring Grove Cemetery in Cincinnati. They had six children. Their house in Newport is a National Historic Landmark. A marker at their grave site was erected in 1902 with funds raised by African American groups. The Coffins lived at 3131 Wehrman Avenue in Cincinnati, a block from the Stowe house. The free trade warehouse was located at Sixth and Elm Streets, a few blocks from the Arnau Center and Fountain Square. The Coffins also owned a few other properties that were known as refuge sites.

SALMON P. CHASE (1808–1873) TO THE DEFENSE OF THE OPPRESSED

Salmon P. Chase was an attorney in Cincinnati who became a senator, governor of Ohio, secretary of the Treasury under Abraham Lincoln and a justice on the U.S. Supreme Court. He was also an ardent abolitionist and represented former slaves who challenged fugitive slave laws. He began his law practice in 1830 in Cincinnati and became friends with Harriet Beecher Stowe and James Birney, among others. He argued that when slaves leave slave states and enter free states, they cease to be slaves. Chase defended many notable slave cases and was known to help and give advice to many fugitives. He helped to purchase and emancipate slaves, such as the well-documented case when he directed Calvin Fairbank to purchase a slave, Eliza, at a notorious auction in Lexington. Chase represented John Van Zandt, who had aided and harbored fugitive slaves, in a U.S. Supreme Court case that challenged the Fugitive Slave Act of 1793.

When a Union supply camp, Camp Nelson, was established in central Kentucky, Abraham Lincoln promised enslaved blacks could be free if they joined the Union forces. Camp Nelson became a muster-in site for many black regiments. As the men fled to join at Camp Nelson, their enslaved families followed, creating a refugee site at the camp within the slave state of Kentucky. It was Salmon P. Chase, with an appeal from John Fee, who issued federal funds to help establish sanitary and safe conditions to take care of these families. Chase was secretary of the Treasury at the time.

JAMES G. BIRNEY (1792–1857)

A native of Danville, Kentucky, Birney was an attorney who moved to Alabama and established a cotton plantation. As a slaveholder, he grew increasingly troubled with the issue of slavery and joined the American Colonization Society. He was disillusioned by the groups ideas and became an ardent supporter for the abolition of slavery. He moved to Cincinnati and operated the *Philanthropist*, an abolitionist newspaper. The printing office was burned down twice during the 1836 race riots in Cincinnati.

Birney moved to New York to work for the American Anti-Slavery Society. Shortly after, he was nominated as the presidential candidate for the antislavery Liberty Party in 1840 and again in 1844. One of his staunch supporters was Henry Bibb. Although Birney was defeated both times, in 1844, it was thought that he drove votes away from the proslavery candidate Henry Clay, who was narrowly defeated by James K. Polk.

THE MARGARET GARNER CASE

The mural of Margaret Garner and her family crossing the Ohio River at the Covington Flood Wall depicts the tragic story of Garner, a fugitive slave, from the A.K. Gaines's Maplewood plantation in Boone County. Margaret and her husband, Robert, along with their four children, escaped one night across the frozen Ohio River at Covington, within a party of seventeen other fugitives. They hid at the home of Joseph Kite in Cincinnati. The other nine fugitives made it safely up town, but unfortunately, the Garner family was captured by Gaines and federal marshals but not before Margaret had slit the throats of her four children. Her two-year-old daughter died, but the other three survived.

A trial was held in Cincinnati. It lasted two weeks, and the verdict was in favor of slaveholder Gaines. John Joliffe, like Salmon Chase in Cincinnati, was known for representing slave fugitives. After the verdict to return Garner to the slaveholder, Joliffe suggested that Margaret should be arrested for murder, which would result in another trial and possibly give Garner another chance for acquittal.

Gaines got wind of the plan and sold the Garner family to his brother in Arkansas. While on the boat downriver, Margaret jumped overboard with her nine-month-old baby in arms. She was rescued by boat hands, but her baby drowned. The family was shipped downriver, and Margaret died of typhoid fever in 1858 while enslaved.[83]

Her story was horrific in several aspects. The idea of a mother killing her children was terrible, but the thought that she would do so as an act of spiritual freedom—to release her children from the brutality of enslavement—captured public sympathy. Her story was captured in the novel *Beloved* by Toni Morrison, which won a Pulitzer Prize.

CALVIN FAIRBANK (1816–1898)

A New York native, Calvin Fairbank aspired to dedicate himself to the abolition of slavery as a very young man. He was an ordained Methodist minister and a graduate of Oberlin College. By the age of twenty-eight, he had assisted more than forty-three slaves across the Ohio River. His story of involvement is all over the Ohio River Valley, stretching from Louisville to Maysville, from Cincinnati to Ripley and to the heartland of Kentucky in Lexington. Fairbank became well-known when he and Delia Webster were captured while returning from assisting slaves Lewis Hayden and his wife, Harriet, and their son, Jo, escape from Lexington to Ripley. For this act, Calvin was sentenced to fifteen years in the Kentucky penitentiary with hard labor—five years for each of the Hayden family members. He received a pardon in 1849 after serving almost five years.

After his pardon, Fairbank went to Cincinnati to work with Levi and Catherine Coffin, Salmon Chase and others. He also became acquainted with Laura Haviland, a Quaker from Michigan, who had started the Raisin Institute and was a friend of Henry Bibb. Against the advice of other abolitionists who feared for her safety, Haviland visited Fairbank when he was imprisoned in Louisville to check on his condition. Fairbank emancipated several slaves in public auction bids that were financed by the Coffins, Chase and others. In his biography, Fairbank described many of the fugitives and the families he helped to freedom.

In 1851, Fairbank was arrested again for aiding the escape of Tamar, a fugitive slave woman from Louisville (see case in chapter 2). As a known abolitionist, he was treated with prejudice and in 1852 was again sentenced to the state penitentiary in Frankfort, where he worked in the hemp factory. He stated that he received 35,105 stripes (whippings) while in prison.

During his imprisonment, his fiancée, Mandana Tileston, moved to Cincinnati, so she could visit him. He received money and "articles of comfort" from Levi Coffin and Laura Haviland. Lewis Hayden, who Fairbank had assisted in escape, had become a prominent businessman, UGRR conductor and political leader in Boston. He raised money for Fairbank on several occasions to try to aid his release. Finally, Lieutenant Governor Richard Jacob, who had always believed Fairbank was unjustly trialed, signed for his release while acting in absence of Governor Bramlette, who was out of state.

Fairbank spent a total of seventeen years and four months in Kentucky prisons for assisting fugitive slaves. When he was pardoned on April 15, 1864, he was warmly welcomed with celebrations and receptions by a host of abolitionist friends. He attended President Lincoln's inauguration in 1865 as a special guest. He continued to speak up for African Americans during the Reconstruction years. Calvin and his wife, Mandana, had a son before she died of tuberculosis in 1876. He remarried Adeline Winger. The years following his release from prison were difficult financially because of his poor health from years of imprisonment. He published his memoirs, *Reverend Calvin Fairbank During Slavery Times: How He Fought the Good Fight to Prepare the Way*, to help finance a living.

JOHN FAIRFIELD

A native of Virginia, John Fairfield grew up in a slaveholding family and despised slavery. He devised a plan to help his close friend Bill, his uncle's slave, escape and go west. The effort was successful, and Fairfield accompanied Bill to Canada. From then on, Fairfield became a conductor for hire, helping fugitives escape at a price.

When he went to an area to help fugitives, he would take on the guise of a shrewd, proslavery businessman, pretending to be interested in buying livestock like cattle or chickens from local farmers. Often, he would stay in the area for a couple of weeks, to blend in.

Levin Coffin became acquainted with Fairfield in Cincinnati. He told Coffin that every slave had a right to freedom and had a perfect right to shoot down anyone who "came between him and liberty."[84] Fairfield himself was heavily armed. He was betrayed several times in his efforts and was arrested and jailed up and down the Ohio River, but he always managed to get out of prison. It was said that he was a high-up member of the order of Freemasons, which helped to secure his release.

At first, Coffin did not believe all of the tales about John Fairfield, but as time went on, he realized that Fairfield was truly a force for the fugitives. He was like a military commander who insisted those he rescued would fight for their lives rather than be captured. In the end, he was known to have rescued hundreds of men, women and children, often leading them to a reunion in Canada.[85]

THE ESCAPE OF THE 28

The Escape of the 28 is an incredible example of John Fairfield's tenacity and courage in leading fugitives to freedom. On the night of April 2, 1853, a group of twenty-eight fugitives, most fleeing from the Parker and Terrill families in Petersburg, Kentucky, met Fairfield at three skiffs tied along the bank of a rain-swollen Ohio River. They crossed the river, even though Fairfield's overcrowded skiff sank, causing him to lead his overcrowded boat through the remainder of the muddy water. The next morning, the fugitives hid in ravines along Mill Creek, near Lawrenceburg, while Fairfield went for help in Cincinnati.[86]

Fairfield enlisted the help of his friend John Hatfield, "a black barber and steamboat steward, whose home was on 5th Street between Race and Elm."[87] Hatfield was a deacon at the well-known abolitionist Zion Baptist Church and a member of the Cincinnati Vigilance Committee, which protected the rights of blacks in the area. A call went out to members of the vigilance committee (including Levi Coffin).

A plan was contrived to retrieve the fugitives by procuring coaches and assembling a funeral procession and slowly moving to the Wesleyan Black Cemetery. From there the group would continue up College Hill, a well-organized community of abolitionists that would further the group's escape. Reverend Jonathon Cable, at College Hill, made arrangements with the ladies of the Anti-Slavery Sewing Society to retrieve clothing from the storeroom at the Levi Coffin house. Coffee, blankets and clothing were taken to the group of twenty-eight, with plans in place.

The journey was successful except for the death of an infant who died in its mother's. Another fugitive joined the group during the event. The group slowly made its way to Canada, staying in free black communities and with Quakers and Wesleyan Methodists along the way. When they reached Detroit, they were greeted by more than two hundred people. They were ferried across the Detroit River by George DeBaptiste, and they were greeted in Canada by conductor Laura Haviland and Henry Bibb. Henry Bibb proudly announced their arrival in his newspaper, *Voice of the Fugitive*, in May 1853, with the heading "Good News from Slavery."

LAURA HAVILAND (1808–1898)

Laura Smith Haviland was raised in Lockport, New York, by parents who were devout Quakers and condemned slavery. She married Charles Haviland in 1825, and they had eight children. The Havilands moved to Michigan, and Laura, with other members of the community, formed the first antislavery organization in Michigan, the Logan Female Anti-Slavery Society, in 1832.

Laura and her husband began the Raisin Institute, which was designed for indigent children, regardless of race, creed or sex. They eventually expanded the school along the traditions of an elementary and high school, hiring a graduate from Oberlin College as the principal.

Laura's husband and one of their children died from an epidemic, and two years later, she lost another child. She was forced to close the Raisin Institute from lack of funds in 1849 but organized the Refugee Home Society, working with her close friend Henry Bibb, as well as George DeBaptiste. Laura Haviland secured funds a few years later and reopened the Raisin Institute by 1856.

She traveled and taught in schools for black children in Cincinnati and Toledo. Laura and her husband had established their home as a stop for refugee slaves on the UGRR. After her husband's death, Haviland began crossing into slave states like Kentucky, Arkansas and Tennessee, risking her own life as a conductor, against the advice of friends, such as Levi and Catherine Coffin, who thought it was too dangerous. One example is the case of John White.

John White had escaped from the Petersburg area in Kentucky and crossed the river to Rising Sun, Indiana, when he learned he was about to be sold South, which would separate him from his wife and children, who were held in bondage by another man. He stayed at the Raisin Institute where he met Laura Haviland. He appealed to Haviland to help him with the escape of his wife and children. Disguising herself, Haviland crossed the river into Kentucky with a group of free black women from Rising Sun to collect blackberries. Laura contacted John's wife to set the plan for escape.

At the appointed time, John White led his family to a skiff bound for Rising Sun, but the Ohio River was swift and carried their small boat downriver from where a wagon was set to meet them. Bounty hunters pursued the group and captured his wife and children, but John got away. John hid for several days before he was captured by sheriff and slave hunter Right Rea from Madison, Indiana. Rea secreted White to a slave jail in Trimble County, Kentucky. White did not reveal his real name to Right and was allowed to send a letter to a friend to ask for help to secure money for his freedom. The letter came into the hands of Laura Haviland, who left for Cincinnati to secure help from Levi Coffin.

Coffin sent his nephew M.C. White to Kentucky, to confirm that it was John White in the Kentucky jail. M.C. White made a contract with Right Rae for $350 to deliver the slave to Cincinnati by boat. Rae delivered John White (not knowing his identity) to Cincinnati early in the morning, and M.C. took John White with the stipulation that he would return the next morning. The next morning, M.C. met Rae at the wharf and informed him that the man was not a slave but a free man and that if Rae took the $350, he would be guilty of kidnapping. Rae took the money, and a writ of corpus was made for the arrest of Right Rae. It was served to Rae in Madison, where he spent some jail time in his own hometown, but a trial never occurred because it would have put John White at risk. John White stayed in Canada and never saw his wife and children again.[88]

There are many other instances when Haviland helped aid and abet fugitives, sometimes in disguise. In 1865, during the Civil War, General Oliver Howard named Haviland as inspector of hospitals for the newly organized Freedmen's Bureau. For the next two years, Haviland traveled through Kansas, Tennessee, Arkansas and other areas, delivering supplies, checking on the conditions of Freedmen and indigent whites, organizing schools and refugee camps and delivering lectures. She would carry "instruments of torture" used on slaves to describe the horrible conditions of slavery.[89] She also helped organize the Women's Christian Temperance Union in Michigan and worked on causes of suffrage for women. Haviland died in Michigan and is buried beside her husband. The town of Haviland, Kansas, was named in her honor because she had done a lot of refugee work there, and a statue of Laura Haviland stands at the Lewanee County Historical Museum in Adrian, Michigan.

THE BARKSHIRE FAMILY OF RISING SUN, INDIANA

The UGRR in Rising Sun was operated by the Barkshire family, originally from Boone County, Kentucky. Samuel Barkshire, born in 1797, was a cooper who was manumitted and opened his cooperage shop in Rising Sun. His former slaveholder, Nancy Hawkins, manumitted the remaining Barkshire family, among others, and moved with them.

Nancy Hawkins joined the Barkshires in Rising Sun and helped conduct freedom seekers as they crossed over the river. All of the Barkshires helped people to safe locations with Samuel's sons, Arthur, Garrett and Woodford, often acting as guides. Nancy Hawkins left her home to the Barkshire sons upon her death in 1854. The home on the corner of Fourth and Poplar Streets continued to operate as a safe house.

JOHN VAN ZANDT (UNKNOWN–1847)

A Fleming County native and former slave owner, Van Zandt was an abolitionist who began conducting fugitives when he moved to Glendale, Ohio. He was captured while assisting nine slaves from Boone County. One of the fugitives, Andrew, escaped, but Van Zandt and the remaining eight were jailed in Covington, Kentucky, and Van Zandt was charged with harboring and concealing fugitives. In 1842, a civil suit was brought by slaveholder Wharton Jones for $450 to pay for the bounty hunters and $500 for the value of the escaped slave Andrew. Cincinnati attorneys Salmon Chase and William Seward represented Van Zandt, and the case was presented before the Supreme Court in 1847. The verdict was in favor of Jones.

Van Zandt became destitute from the legal fees. Van Zandt was also excommunicated from the Sharonville Methodist Church that he founded in Ohio, which contended that aiding fugitive slaves was ungodly. The church reversed its decision in 2006, 163 years later.[90] Van Zandt was one of the conductors who Harriet Beecher Stowe used as a model for her character Van Trompe in *Uncle Tom's Cabin*.

SCENIC ROUTES

Continue along the Ohio River Scenic Byway: From Vevay, take State Road 156, which rejoins State Road 56 through Rising Sun and Aurora. From Aurora, connect to Highway 50 through Lawrenceburg. After Lawrenceburg, Highway 50 connects to the 275 Bypass at Cincinnati.

PLACES TO VISIT

INDIANA SIDE

Ohio County

Rising Sun

A case was tried at the Rising Sun Courthouse when Arthur Barkshire, a free person of color, married a free woman of color, Elizabeth Keith, and brought her to live at his home in Rising Sun after Article 8 of the Indiana Constitution was passed in 1851. The article restricted any free person of color from moving into the state as a permanent resident. Barkshire was fined by officials in Ohio County and appealed the case to the Indiana Supreme Court, which ruled against Barkshire. The house is located at the corner of Fourth and Poplar Streets in Rising Sun. The Rising Sun Courthouse was built in 1844–45 and is still in use today, making it the oldest courthouse in continuous use in the Hoosier State. See staff at the Ohio County Historical Museum for more information on the Barkshires.

Address: 413 Main Street, Rising Sun, Indiana

Ohio County Historical Museum

The Ohio County Historical Museum in Rising Sun is housed in a nineteenth-century plow factory and displays local family collections from the 1800s and early 1900s. The best-known item is the 1920s hydroplane racing boat *Hoosier Boy*. There is also local information on UGRR activities and sites in the area, including Barkshire Family information.

Website: www.ohiocountyhistory.org
Address: 212 South Walnut Street, Rising Sun, Indiana
Phone: (812) 438-4915

Former slaves from Boone County, the Barkshire family, moved across the river at Rising Sun and were UGRR conductors with their former slaveholder, Nancy Hawkins. *Author's collection.*

The waterfront of Rising Sun, Indiana, as seen from Rabbit Hash in Boone County, Kentucky. The Ohio County Historical Society in Rising Sun has exhibits and information on the UGRR. *Author's collection.*

Dearborn County

Lawrenceburg

Lawrenceburg is known as the route that the members of the Escape of the 28 took on their journey to Canada. It was also the home of Elijah Anderson after he moved from Madison, Indiana. After his move from Madison to Lawrenceburg, Elijah Anderson was known to set up major routes on the Underground Railroad out of Boone County through Cincinnati. He earned the name of the Superintendent of the Underground Railroad and assisted large groups of fugitives. His final arrest was in Bedford in Trimble County for helping a young boy name George run away. The testimony of Sheriff Right Rea resulted in an eight-year prison sentence in Kentucky. On the day of his release, Elijah Anderson was found dead in his prison cell.

Aurora

The Aurora Ferry connecting Kentucky and Indiana from 1819 until the 1990s. The ornate Hillforest Mansion was built by Thomas Gaff, a shipping merchant on the Ohio River. With its proximity to Lawrenceburg, UGRR conductor Elijah Anderson worked in this area to direct fugitives north along the Indiana State Road 350 to Old Milan and along the railroad tracks.

The Lawrenceburg Historic District was an escape site where conductor Elijah Anderson helped fugitives along the URGG. Anderson moved to Lawrenceburg from Madison and became known as Superintendent of the UGRR. *Author's collection.*

OHIO

Cincinnati

The National Underground Railroad Freedom Center

The wharf area of Cincinnati, the first step on free soil for many, is now the home to the National Underground Railroad Museum Freedom Center, which houses a reconstructed Anderson Slave Jail that was removed from Mason County, Kentucky (see discussion of Anderson in chapter 5). Nestled between the Bengals and Reds stadiums overlooking the Ohio River, the center offers excellent exhibits on topics of slavery with many current-day topics on black history and civil rights. This museum is a high priority for a visit and gives important connections between slavery of the past and its profound impact in today's society.

The movie *Brothers of the Borderland* is based on the abolitionists of Ripley, Ohio, in particular John Rankin and John Parker (included in chapter 5). The *Suite for Freedom* is another powerful series of three animated films on slavery. The center has temporary exhibits and featured educational programs throughout the year that feature inspirational stories of freedom

The Anderson Slave Jail is the featured exhibit at the National UGRR Freedom Center Museum on the Cincinnati waterfront. The slave jail documents the activities of John Anderson and his slave trade from his farm in Mason County. *Author's collection.*

seekers from the past to current day. The museum overlooks a newly renovated waterfront space with spray fountains, restaurants, an indoor carousel and a large Ferris wheel. The historic Roebling Bridge offers a way to cross over the Ohio River to Covington, connecting to the Robert Dafford Murals and the historic Riverside Drive in Covington. This museum is unique and gives insight for experiencing the impact of the UGRR on the Ohio River. There is an admission charge.

Website: www.freedomcenter.org
Address: 50 East Freedom Way, Cincinnati, Ohio
Phone: (513) 333-7739

Salmon P. Chase Historical Marker

This marker is located just across the bridge from the Great American Ball Park on the corner of East Third Street, almost directly across from the Freedom Center. Chase was an UGRR conductor, governor of Ohio, secretary of the Treasury under Abraham Lincoln and the sixth chief justice of the Supreme Court (1864–1873). Chase defended runaway slaves and those who harbored them. He was a friend of Harriet Beecher Stowe, Levi and Catherine Coffin, Calvin Fairbanks and James Birney, among others.

Spring Grove Cemetery and Arboretum

UGRR Conductors Levi and Catherine Coffin and Salmon Chase are buried in the Spring Grove Cemetery. The funerals of all three of these notable people were attended and honored by former slaves and friends of the UGRR. The cemetery was created when numbers of deaths resulting from the cholera epidemic created a need for larger spaces for burial in the 1830s. Members of the Cincinnati Horticultural Society formed a cemetery association in 1844, which resulted in today's expansive burial ground of 733 acres containing a beautifully landscaped collection of native and exotic plants. Salmon Chase prepared the articles of corporation to charter this nonprofit nondenominational corporation in 1845. The Gothic limestone sanctuaries, chapels and fencing add to the sacred and grand nature of the setting.

Website: www.springgrove.org
Address: 4521 Spring Grove Avenue, Cincinnati, Ohio
Phone: (513) 681-7526

Spring Grove Cemetery is the burial site for UGRR conductors Levi and Catherine Coffin and Samuel Chase. The cemetery, composed of 733 acres, is on the National Register of Historic Places and includes an extensive arboretum and unusual monuments. *Author's collection.*

Harriet Beecher Stowe House

Harriet Beecher was twenty-one when her father, Reverend Lyman Beecher, moved the family from Connecticut to this house in Cincinnati, to assume the presidency of the Lane Theological Seminary (located nearby but no longer extant). Harriet married Calvin Stowe, who was a professor at Lane, and they settled into their home on nearby Gilbert Avenue (no longer extant). Harriet lived in this now beautifully restored home before her marriage and at different times with her children when her husband was away on business. The home is on the National Register of Historic Places and the National Park Service National Underground Railroad Network. Interpreters provide programs throughout the year and will help suggest other landmarks to visit.

Website: www.ohiohistory.org/stowe
Address: 2950 Gilbert Avenue, Cincinnati, Ohio
Phone: (800) 847-6507

The Harriet Beecher Stowe House Museum shows Stowe's life when she lived in Cincinnati. It includes daily tours and extensive information about the UGRR activities in Cincinnati. *Author's collection.*

College Hill

College Hill is a residential area of Cincinnati that is perched high on a ridge overlooking the city and the Ohio River Valley. The are many sites along the main road, Hamilton Avenue, that are a piece of the history on the UGRR in this area. Some of these sites are listed with the National Park Service National Underground Railroad Network. The Six Acres Bed and Breakfast at 5350 Hamilton Avenue is one of the sites listed as a safe house. It was built by Zebulon Strong as fugitives came up the east ravine on their escape route through Cincinnati. There was also a free black community in the East Cedar Avenue area. The members of the Escape of the 28 hid in the Wesleyan Cemetery on their way through town. This online brochure will help guide you through the area: www.hamiltonavenueroadtofreedom.org.

The Cincinnati Museum Center—Cincinnati History Museum

In 2018, the Cincinnati Museum Center completed a multimillion-dollar renovation in the old Union Train terminal. This is a multi-museum complex featuring the Cincinnati History Museum, Duke Energy Children's Museum,

This *Public Landing* exhibit at the Cincinnati Museum Center features life at the wharf landing in Cincinnati during the 1850s. *Author's collection.*

Museum of Natural History and Science, Linder Family Omnimax Theatre and Wolf Holocaust and Human Center. They have recently completed an exhibit called *Public Landing* that shows how the Cincinnati riverfront looked during the 1800s, with stores, the wharf and many hands-on activities that put you back in pre–Civil War life on the river. There are exhibits on dinosaurs and space and a great children's museum where kids wander through all types of challenging activities. There is a nice food area with healthy food choices and drinks. This museum complex can be an entire day's visit.

Website: www.cincymuseum.org
Address: 1301 Western Avenue, Cincinnati, Ohio
Phone: (513) 287-7000

Fountain Square

Fountain Square marks the vicinity that was the hub of activity in the wharf area. The street was lined with taverns, hotels and questionable activities, and it was a place where fugitives could find quick sanctuary

Fountain Square in downtown Cincinnati was the center of activity during the UGRR years. There were brothels, taverns and easy hide outs that lined the streets in this area for fugitives to disappear. *Author's collection.*

during escape. UGRR operators Levi and Catherine Coffin operated the free trade warehouse at Sixth and Elm Streets. There was a free press bookstore and the Ladies Anti-Slavery Sewing Circle at the corner of Walnut and Sixth Streets. Today, this area features some of the top restaurants in Cincinnati, as well as many hotels. There are several activities scheduled at the nearby Aronoff Center and concerts on weekends. It is within easy walking distance of the Freedom Center and the Bengals and Reds stadiums

Address: 520 Vine Street, Cincinnati, Ohio

Findlay Market

Findlay Market is one of the oldest markets in the United States in continuous use (erected in 1852) and was voted one of the best public markets in the United States. During the early 1800s, it formed the northern boundary of Cincinnati and attracted a concentration of bootleggers, entrepreneurs, saloons, gambling houses, dance halls, brothels and other institutions not tolerated in the city proper. Findlay

Findlay Market was an escape route as fugitives headed toward the UGRR route to College Hill. *Author's collection.*

Market provided another easy escape for fugitives to blend in to a busy, public area. Findlay was on the route for fugitives on their journey to College Hill and north. Before the Civil War, Cincinnati operated nine public markets, which were a primary source of perishable food, including butchers and fish sellers. Today, the market offers traditional meats from German heritage, as well as a wide and varied assortment of foods, restaurants and crafts. It is open Tuesday through Sunday.

Website: www.findlaymarket.org
Address: 1801 Race Street, Cincinnati, Ohio

New Richmond, Ohio and Clermont County

With its proximity to Cincinnati, New Richmond was a very well-known abolitionist town and community. There is a great tour guide developed by Clermont County called the Freedom Trail, which lists nineteen sites on the National Park Service National Underground Railroad Network. Several of these sites are in the river town of New Richmond, including the Cransion Memorial Presbyterian Church and the site of James Birney's printing house

Cranston Memorial Presbyterian Church was the site where the New Richmond Anti-Slavery Society held candlelight meetings as early as 1836. *Author's collection.*

for his abolitionist newspaper the *Philanthropist*. Other notable sites in Clermont County are the various sites that honor the activities of the Fee Family (relatives of abolitionist John Gregory Fee from Augusta).

Website: www.discoverclermont.com/freedomtrail

KENTUCKY

Boone County

Boone County Library UGRR Tours

The main branch of the Boone County Library is conveniently located off the I-71, I-75 exchange at 1786 Burlington, Kentucky. This county borders the section of the Ohio River across from Rising Sun, Aurora and Lawrenceburg, Indiana, which are documented sites for fugitives and UGRR conductors. The Boone County Public Library has an UGRR driving tour that can be picked up at the library. The tour will take you by the

The Dinsmore House in Boone County recreates the lives of the Dinsmore family, whose tenants and slaves raised produce and livestock for the Cincinnati markets. *Author's collection.*

Dinsmore House (preserved and documented slaveholding household with a cemetery that is open to the public), as well as documented escape sites (the famous 28 near Rabbit Hash and John White family at Petersburg). This tour is on the National Park Service National Underground Railroad Network. The library also offers UGRR tours—call to schedule for small or large groups.

Website: www.bcpl.org
Address: 1786 Burlington Pike, Burlington, Kentucky
Phone: (859) 342-2665

Covington and Newport Area—Licking River

Licking Riverside Neighborhood

James Bradley came to America from Africa as an infant. By the age of eighteen, he had earned enough money to purchase his freedom from an Arkansas plantation. He enrolled in Lane Seminary in Cincinnati and

This James Bradley statue on Riverside Drive in Covington acknowledges Bradley, who purchased his freedom as a young man and attended Lane Seminary. *Author's collection.*

participated in the Lane Seminary debates where he declared that the desire of slaves was "liberty and education." A statue of Bradley is found in the Historic Licking Riverside neighborhood in Covington at the corner of the Licking River, facing the Ohio River. It is recognized as one of the premiere historic districts in the Cincinnati area and was voted one of the ten great neighborhoods in 2013 by the American Planning Association (APA).

A walk through the neighborhood reveals every major evolutionary style of American architecture from 1815 through 1920. The Thomas Carneal house (circa 1815) on Kennedy Street has a tunnel that leads from the Licking River to the house, which was used to transport goods. When the Carneals were away (they had a home in Lexington, Kentucky), it was thought that the tunnel was used for the UGRR. The neighborhood association has taken great pride in the restoration. There are numerous statues honoring iconic figures (such as Bradley) placed along a walkway facing the Cincinnati waterfront, which includes a small park. The neighborhood is adjacent to the Roebling Bridge.

The Roebling Murals at the Covington Riverfront by Robert Dafford

The Roebling Murals at the Covington Riverfront are a series of eighteen panels depicting the history of Covington from 800 B.C. to present day. The murals are on the floodwall facing the Cincinnati riverfront. Robert Dafford is the mural artist and has painted other murals on floodwalls in Paducah and Maysville, Kentucky. Dafford, who resides in Louisana, is internationally known for his murals, which are found in many places in the United States. *The Flight of the Garner Family* portrays Margaret Garner and her family in their flight from slavery as they crossed the frozen Ohio River to reach Cincinnati from Covington. Garner's story inspired the Pulitzer Prize–winning book *Beloved* by Toni Morrison. Other

The Garner Family Escapes is a part of the history mural series by Robert Dafford on the floodwall in Covington by the Roebling Bridge. *Author's collection.*

murals show a herd of buffalo following the trace that formed Kentucky's early pioneer roads, as well as Civil War soldiers crossing the Ohio on a pontoon bridge.

Website: www.covingtonky.gov

Mainstrasse Village in Covington: Garner Historical Marker

This pre–Civil War village was settled by German and Irish immigrants and underwent a revitalization effort in the 1970s as a tourist destination storybook German village. There is a Margaret Garner Historical Marker placed at the intersection of Main and Sixth Streets to indicate the path the Garner's would have taken to cross the river into Cincinnati when she and her family were fleeing to Cincinnati.

Behringer Crawford Museum

Located in Devou Park, high on a ridge overlooking the Ohio River Valley, the Behringer Crawford Museum has permanent displays on natural history, archaeology, paleontology, rivers and steamboats, frontier home life, the Civil War and slavery. Special temporary exhibits are featured throughout the year. It has hands-on activities for children and is open Tuesday through Saturday. There is an admission charge.

Website: www.bcmuseum.org
Address: 1600 Montague Road, Covington, Kentucky
Phone: (859) 491-4003

James A. Ramage Civil War Museum

The James A. Ramage Civil War Museum is located on the site of Battery Hooper. Battery Hooper is one of the few remaining Civil War defensive positions left in the region where men, women and children worked together to erect an eight-mile defensive line from Ludlow to Fort Thomas to defend against the Confederate invasion of Kentucky. Men of the Black Brigade of Cincinnati were credited for their work on the project. When eight thousand Confederate soldiers marched into the area, they were impressed by the defensive actions and withdrew their offense during the night. The museum is on a fourteen-acre park that provides an impressive view and overlook of the region. Open on Friday, Saturday and Sunday.

Website: www.fortwright.com
Address: 1402 Highland Avenue, Fort Wright, Kentucky
Phone: (859) 344-1145

5

A COMMUNITY CONNECTED

Ripley and Point Pleasant, Ohio, and Augusta,
Washington and Maysville, Kentucky

The Ohio-Kentucky routes probably served more fugitives than others in the North.
—*Wilbur Siebert*

The Maysville-Lexington Turnpike that connects Lexington, Kentucky, to the Ohio River at Maysville Kentucky (formerly called Limestone Trace), was an old buffalo trace worn down by the bison herds that once frequented the area. There were natural salt licks along the path that attracted wildlife and settlers. The trace directed traders and settlers coming down the Ohio River to the rich bluegrass soils of central Kentucky. The turnpike was "the first road west of the Alleghenies to be 'macadamized,' significant improvement that involved layering the road-bed with six-ounce stones."[91] The sixty-four-mile road included six covered bridges and thirteen tollhouses and passed from Lexington through Paris, Millersburg and Washington before ending at the Ohio River in Maysville. It took five days to make the trip from Maysville to Lexington. It was the most direct route from Lexington to the Ohio for sending produce and commodities, including slaves, to the southern markets.[92]

While Louisville may have been known for its slave trading and holding jails, Lexington was known for its large public auctions that attracted hundreds. There are many recorded stories and eyewitness events where coffles of slaves were chained in gangs both for the public and private auctions in Lexington. Slaves were sometimes unloaded from riverboats

This old road marker on display at the Harriet Beecher Stowe Museum indicates the significance of the old pioneer road from Maysville to the inner bluegrass region to Lexington. *Author's collection.*

in Maysville and then walked down the Maysville-Lexington Turnpike to Lexington for auction. Public auctions were held on "court days" at Cheapside in Lexington, not far from the courthouse. Robards was a slave trader in the area and was known to scour the countryside, collecting human chattel for private sales in his Lexington jail.[93]

These slave traders and agents often needed temporary housing as they gathered more "human chattel" before shipment. In Louisville, Henry Bibb discussed how slave trader Mathew Garrison used the Louisville jail and workhouse to hold slaves as he gathered enough for a profitable shipment to New Orleans. In Mason County, at a farm outside Germantown, Captain John W. Anderson provided a snapshot of a slave trader within a small rural community.

THE ANDERSON SLAVE JAIL

The Anderson Slave Jail was located near Germantown in Mason County about nine miles from the Ohio River at John W. Anderson's farm. Anderson, a slave trader for ten years prior to his death in 1834, bought slaves in the local area either at auction or privately and kept them in his jail until he had enough to profit from shipping them south on the Ohio River or overland to the Natchez markets. The two-story jail placed men and boys, chained to each other, on the second floor, with women and small children living below. There would have been no privacy in the unsanitary conditions, with worse circumstances imaginable. Anderson worked in partnership with others in the trade.[94]

From various local sources and oral traditions, and through research and archaeology, the Anderson Slave Jail became a publicly known site. During the same time, the National Underground Railroad Freedom Center in Cincinnati was being designed, and the Anderson Slave Jail was moved to the center for the centerpiece exhibit. Today, the Anderson Slave Jail is an

This serene setting is the site of the John Anderson farm where a slave jail moved to the National UGRR Freedom Center in Cincinnati for interpretation on slave history and trade. *Author's collection.*

educational tool that demonstrates the reality of the slave trade and stands as testimony to the destruction and cruelty forced upon innocent people.

Researchers and writers since the Anderson Slave Jail story have come upon other instances where local operators of slave jails and traders, like Anderson, existed in Kentucky. Lucien Rule, a historian from Oldham County, collected stories about a man named Ralph Tarleton, who participated in slave trading, even sending his own offspring from his harem of slaves, downriver to markets.[95]

LEWIS HAYDEN (1811–1889)

Enslaved in Lexington, Kentucky, Hayden was inspired at age fourteen when he attended a parade that was given in honor of the Marquette de Lafayette. Lafayette tipped his hat to the young man as he walked by and at that moment, Hayden realized his self-worth as a human and not as someone's property and chattel. Hayden's first wife, Esther Harvey, and their son were enslaved by US senator Henry Clay, who sold them downriver.

Hayden never saw them again. He remarried Harriet Bell and they had a son, Joseph. By that time Hayden could read and write, he had made appeals to UGRR conductors for a plan of escape. UGRR conductors Calvin Fairbank and Delia Webster worked with the Hayden family for a successful escape to freedom through Washington and Maysville, crossing the Ohio River (probably at Sutton Street in Maysville). Fairbank and Webster were arrested on their return to Lexington.

Hayden and Harriet made it to Canada and founded a church of the Colored Methodist Society and a school for black children. They later moved to Boston and their home became a part of the Underground Railroad where a number of people received safe shelter between 1850 and 1860. Harriet Beecher Stowe visited with the Haydens and witnessed thirteen fugitives at the Hayden house. Calvin Fairbank was often a guest at their home.

Lewis Hayden was an active Freemason and successful businessman in Boston. He was elected as representative to the Massachusetts state legislature. He was a recruiter for the Fifty-Fourth Regiment of the US Colored Troupes for the Union during the Civil War. His son, Joseph, was killed serving in the Union navy. He and his wife Harriet left their estate of $5,000 to Harvard University for scholarships for African American medical students.

WASHINGTON, MASON COUNTY: A FRONTIER TOWN

From the river landing at Maysville (formerly called Limestone), travelers took a four-mile road inland to the frontier town of Washington. By 1790, Washington had close to five hundred residents and offered taverns and lodging to travelers bound to the Bluegrass region of Lexington. Today, many of the town's original Federal- and Georgian-style homes have been preserved. Harriet Beecher Stowe stayed at the Marshal Key house in Washington with a college friend, Miss Dutton, and Key's daughter, who was a student of Stowe's. This is one of the places where Stowe witnessed a public slave auction.

When UGRR conductors Calvin Fairbank and Delia Webster transported fugitive slaves Lewis Hayden and his family from Lexington to the Ohio River at Maysville, they passed through Washington. The tavern owner at 2013 Old Main Street in Washington, H.G. Musack, was witness for the prosecution. He reported seeing them "flee through the town during the wee hours" when they ferreted the Hayden family to the Ohio River. On the way back, they rented a room from Musack.[96]

The Marshal house now serves as the Harriet Beecher Stowe Museum. Marshal Key was one of the major slave owners of Mason County, retaining anywhere between seventeen and thirty slaves, according to the federal census between 1810 and 1850. There are numerous displays on Stowe as well as other information about the UGRR and the frontier town of Washington. Also included is a tobacco press that was designed and patented by John Parker. Parker was a free black and a known UGRR conductor in Ripley, Ohio. Parker's story is further detailed in this chapter under the Ripley, Ohio section.

ELIZA HARRIS

Eliza Harris and her husband, George, were fugitive slaves from Mason County. Eliza is believed to have fled from slaveholder John G. Bacon in Mason County at the junction of Tuckahoe and South Ripley Roads.[97] They reached a safe place in central Ohio at the home of former Ripley, Ohio resident Reverend William Dunlap. In this venture, Eliza had to leave her infant behind. A few months later, during the height of a severe winter, Eliza returned to the plantation to get her child. The Ohio River was partially frozen, and the temperature was below zero. Successfully retrieving her infant, Eliza was stuck on the Kentucky side of the river hiding in some bushes. A man found the pair and took them in that night, when, in the light of morning, Eliza woke to the sound of baying hounds and slave catchers.

With babe in arms, Eliza crossed the partially frozen river, using a small pole for balance. Eliza was helped up the frozen bank by Ripley local Chancy Shaw. Shaw, who was part of the patrol searching for Eliza, said, "Any woman who crossed that river, carrying her baby, has won her freedom."[98] Shaw showed her the way to Reverend John Rankin's house. From there, Eliza and her child were assisted safely to Canada through the efforts of John Van Zandt and Levi Coffin.[99]

Eliza's efforts to help others escape continued. She wanted to return to Kentucky to bring her children and grandchildren to free soil. Reverend Rankin thought her plan was too dangerous, so she enlisted the help of a French Canadian who secured boats for the fugitives on the Kentucky side. Dressing as a man, Eliza entered the Davis farm where her family was enslaved. At the proper time, the fugitives fled to the river but had missed the French Canadian, so they all hid in the corn fields that night. The next day, the man arrived with the skiffs and the group crossed into Ripley. At this point, slave hunters and posse were in pursuit. John Rankin estimated that there were thirty slave hunters giving chase. The group hid under the security of the families in the Ripley area for two weeks before being taken to a Quaker settlement and ferreted to Canada.[100]

There have been several other stories that describe the escape of Eliza Harris. Her bravery and dramatic escape across the frozen Ohio River became legendary. UGRR conductors Levi Coffin and John Rankin also describe author Caroline Miller's version of the Harris story, her escapes and her efforts of guiding members of her family to freedom. Harriet Beecher Stowe modeled her character Eliza in *Uncle Tom's Cabin* after Eliza Harris.

AUGUSTA, KENTUCKY

An array of early nineteenth-century estate homes line Riverside Drive along the Ohio River in historic Augusta. The feeling of a pioneer town resonates in the brick-lined streets in this town founded in 1786 as a trading post. Several of the oldest structures in Kentucky are found here: the 1811 jail that includes an interior log-holding cell and the nearby Baker-Bird Winery, thought to be the oldest commercial estate winery in the United States. Since April 2, 1798, a ferry has shuttled passengers back and forth between the Kentucky and Ohio shores. This town holds a lot of interest for the UGRR because of well-known abolitionists who lived and worked here, such as John and Matilda Fee and the Thome family.

Augusta College, chartered in 1822 as a liberal arts Methodist college, was very active in debates on slavery and colonization. No longer extant, the current Augusta public school sits on the site of the former college. A dormitory for the college is across the street and is currently being restored by the Bracken County Historical Society.

The Battle of Augusta took place here in 1862 when Colonel Basil Duke led seven companies of Confederate soldiers to Cemetery Hill, which overlooked the town. Joshua Bradford had a Union militia of 125 men stationed in Augusta at the time. Duke's forces were met with large resistance both from the Union militia and local townspeople. In this battle, 75 Confederate soldiers were killed, while only 15 Union soldiers were killed.

JAMES ARMSTRONG THOME (1813–1873)

James Thome was born in Augusta in the family home called White Hall. He was the son of Arthur Thome (1769–1855). Thome attended Augusta College, then went to Lane Seminary in Cincinnati to complete his degree. He became an avid abolitionist, convincing his father, a slaveholder, to emancipate their slaves. Arthur Thome then became a conductor for the UGRR, later moving his family to Missouri where he continued to help fugitives. James went on to become vice-president of the Anti-Slavery Society, helping to organize the 1834 American Anti-Slavery Convention and making public addresses denouncing slavery. James became a professor at Oberlin College.[101]

THE REVEREND JOHN GREGG FEE (1816–1901) AND HIS WIFE, MATILDA HAMILTON FEE (1824–1895)

Reverend John Fee and his wife, Matilda Hamilton Fee, are extraordinary figures from the abolitionist movement in Kentucky. Born in Bracken County, Fee's father, John, was a slaveholder, of which John was vehemently opposed. John's mother, Sarah Gregg, came from a family of Quakers who were opposed to slavery.[102] John attended Augusta College, Lane Seminary and Miami College of Ohio. After his graduation from Lane, he was ordained as a minister by Harmony Presbytery in Kentucky. He became an associate of the American Missionary Society and planted his church, the Free Church and School, on Hillsdale Road (for blacks and whites) near Germantown, not far from where he was born.

The American Missionary Society sent William Haines, a colporteur, to assist Fee. Haines was aggressive in delivering abolitionist materials around the Maysville area and was arrested for his activities. A trial took place and eventually reached a verdict of not guilty, but in the process, Fee was brutally attacked—one of several times during Fee's abolitionist years. While the Fees lived in the Mason County area, there was a noticeable number of slave escapes or emancipations.

John Fee became friends with Cassius Clay, and in 1853, he organized the Union Church in Berea, then with financial assistance from Clay, Fee founded Berea College, a school founded to accept both black and white students. Slave supporters grew leery of Fee and accused him of supporting slave risings, such as the Harpers Ferry Arsenal raid that was instigated by John Brown. Brown's raid had epitomized the fears of slave owners who were worried about slave insurrections in their own communities.

John and Matilda continued to conduct services and host other colporteurs sponsored by the American Missionary Society. Matilda's parents, Vincent and Betsy Hamilton, also hosted colporteurs and provided sanctuary for fugitives. When Fee appeared for sermons and talks at churches, there were often angry mobs that threatened Fee's life and livelihood. At one time, he received a sharp blow to his head. At another time, his horse was taken and shaved to the tail. At still other times, mobs escorted him and threatened to lynch him.[103]

During the Civil War, John Fee helped fugitive families that fled to Camp Nelson in central Kentucky. When Abraham Lincoln established the Camp Nelson supply camp for the Union outside Nicholasville, it became a muster-in site for slaves. Lincoln promised that slaves would be free if they joined the Union. As the men became soldiers, their families followed them to Camp Nelson—in part from fear of retribution from slaveholders and as a chance to live on free soil in the middle of a slave state. Numbers of refugee families grew, and it was John Fee who arrived to set up camps, schools, kitchens and medical facilities to aid the families. When the supplies reached a critical point, Fee appealed to Cincinnati attorney Salmon Chase, for federal funds. Chase, the appointed treasurer for Abraham Lincoln, sent funds for the fugitive families at Camp Nelson. (See more about Chase in chapter 4.)

JULIET MILES

The Miles case is one that shows the extreme attitudes in the Fee family regarding slavery. Juliet Miles (1811–1861) was a friend and caretaker of John Gregory Fee as he was growing up. She was enslaved by John Gregory's father, John. Fee purchased Miles and emancipated Juliet and her son, Henry, in 1851. They moved to Felicity, Ohio, sixteen miles from her enslaved family in Kentucky. Miles had four children in Ohio, but she had left ten children and grandchildren enslaved in Kentucky.

In 1858, Juliet Miles was arrested and captured at the banks of the Ohio River, close to Augusta, when she attempted to help her enslaved children and grandchildren escape. Matilda and her children were thrown in the local jail. Both Matilda and John Fee spoke up for Juliet but to no avail. James Fee,

John G. Fee's brother, who owned the enslaved children, sold them, and they were shipped to the New Orleans slave markets. Miles spent a cold winter in the local Bracken County jail, and in her trial in February, she was sentenced to three years in the Kentucky penitentiary. The case was highly publicized in the *New York Daily Tribune*. John and Matilda Fee visited Juliet Miles at the state penitentiary. Miles was said to have "pined" herself to death and died in prison after serving two years.[104]

RIPLEY, OHIO: A TOWN CONNECTED WITH ABOLITIONISTS

Ripley, Ohio, was founded by Revolutionary War soldier and surveyor Colonel Poage, who claimed this part of the Northwest Territory along the Ohio River. His first claims were in Kentucky, but he abhorred slavery and settled across from the slave state, in Ohio, along the rich acreage formed from the river bottomland. Others soon followed, many with a hatred of slavery, and settled in this small community of Ripley. Situated between Maysville and Augusta, Kentucky, and fifty-five miles upstream from Cincinnati, Ripley became a busy port for ship builders, pork packers, woolen mills and other products. It also became a place for runaway slaves.

Nearby and north of Ripley were several black communities whose founders had been part of a group of 950 slaves freed by Samuel Gist. Gist, a very wealthy man, stipulated in his will that his estate would support the purchase of land in Virginia for freed slaves, but the state legislature was against this, citing an 1806 law that allowed manumission only if slaves left the state. Three hundred of the Gist group left Virginia and settled in two communities in Brown County, Ohio.[105]

The scene was set at Ripley for a perfect UGRR community that could help refugees flee slave states and settle in the North. The free black communities acted as a disguise for hiding fugitives, and several families in Ripley became staunch activists, including John Rankin and John Parker.

JOHN PARKER (1827–1900)

John Parker was born into slavery in Norfolk, Virginia. He was the son of a white man and black woman. At the age of eight, he was forced to walk from Norfolk to Richmond in chains bound to another slave. He was then sold, and he marched in chains to Mobile, Alabama. He bought his freedom in 1845, earning money from his skills learned at a foundry in Alabama.

After obtaining his freedom, Parker first moved to New Albany, Indiana, then Cincinnati where he became involved in helping fugitives escape from bondage. By 1848, he had married Miranda Boulton, a Cincinnati native. They then moved to Ripley, Ohio, a place where Parker could open his own iron foundry while working with abolitionists such as Reverend John Rankin, Senator Alexander Campbell and other conductors from Ripley and the nearby Gist communities.

Through the next fifteen years, leading up to the Civil War, Parker aided slaves by night across the Ohio River and worked his foundry and machine shop during the day. After the war, Parker expanded his business. Even among setbacks such as fire and financial crisis, he continued, building the Phoenix Foundry with patents on several inventions.

The Parkers's children all received higher education, with two of his sons, Hale and Cassius, attending Oberlin College Preparatory School. His three daughters, Bianca, Portia and Hortense, studied music. Hortense Parker became one of the first African American graduates from Mount Holyoke College. Another son, Horatio, was a school principal and later a postal clerk.

The Parker family, children included, just like the John Rankin family, all participated in rescuing fugitives and harboring them in their home. In Parker's autobiography, he states that he assisted 440 fugitives on their way to Canada and had a bounty on his head in Kentucky for "$1000, Dead or Alive"[106] In the following, Parker gives a general description of the fugitive slaves he helped:

The early fall was the time that most of them [fugitives] *who were intelligent and determined decided to break away from their bondage. There were cornfields for food and the ground was hard and more difficult to track. As soon as the food supply* [corn had ripened] *they were off. They always started with a bag of provisions and a load of unnecessary things. These were thrown away, until he got down to his knapsack of food. Men and women whom I helped on their way came from Tennessee, requiring weeks to make the journey, sleeping under the trees in the daytime and slowly picking their dangerous way at night...they became backswoodsmen, following the North Star, or even mountains, to reach their destination, the*

Ohio River. Once there, they felt they were in view of their promised land, even if they had no way to cross into it....These long-distance travelers were usually people strong physically, as well as people of character, and were resourceful when confronted with trouble, otherwise they could have never escaped.[107]

JOHN RANKIN (1793-1886)

A light burned day and night from the John and Jean Rankin house in Ripley Ohio, acting as a beacon for fugitives. The powerful symbol of the house and light cannot be experienced until you visit the panoramic point where the Rankin home stands 540 feet high on a ridge with an expanse of miles, both east and west, overlooking the Ohio River.

A native of Jefferson County, Tennessee, Rankin attended Washington College, where he met his wife, Jean Lowry. They married in 1816, and in 1817, Rankin became an ordained Presbyterian minister. Jean was an accomplished seamstress and together they began a career in church service, raising a family of thirteen children and becoming conductors on the UGRR.

The Rankins were abolitionists, which caused anguish and stress from Rankin's proslavery congregations in northern Kentucky. Rankin preached in Lexington, Paris, Cynthiana, Carlyle, Mount Pleasant, Mayslick, Flemingsburg, Maysville and Augusta. The family moved to Ripley, Ohio, in 1822, and John became pastor at two Presbyterian churches—the one at Ripley and another at Strait Creek. From there he also planted other churches around the community. One of Rankin's brothers, Thomas, was a slave owner in Virginia, which prompted John Rankin to write a series of letters to him on the evils of slavery. These compositions were compiled into a book titled *Letters on American Slavery*. It was published in Ripley by John Rankin in 1826 and became one of the earliest antislavery books in the United States. The letters were so controversial that a warehouse where some of them were housed was destroyed by suspected arsonists.

John Rankin was a member of the American Anti-Slavery Society and was often confronted by mobs when he gave public addresses. The Rankins purchased farmland high on the hill that overlooked Ripley and the Ohio River. A large lantern burned each night as a signal to fugitive slaves. In addition, Rankin constructed a staircase leading up the steep hill from

Ripley to their home for slaves to climb up to safety. There was never a slave that was captured in the Rankin home. Rankin, Parker, Campbell and others worked together in Ripley, and the area became famous for its work on the UGRR.

John Rankin, along with Alexander Campbell and Archibald Liggett, founded the College of Ripley in 1828. It allowed black students, such as Benjamin Franklin Templeton, to attend. However, racial tensions forced Templeton to transfer to Hanover College. Ulysses Grant attended the college from 1838 to 1839, until he transferred to West Point.

Like John Parker, there was a bounty on Rankin's head and bounty hunters were thwarted several times at Rankin's home. In one instance, John's son Calvin was fired at while he was pursing six men running away from the Rankin house and barn. The bullet nearly missed him

The Rankins were friends of Harriet Beecher Stowe's parents, and the Beechers stayed with the Rankins in Ripley during a meeting of the Cincinnati Synod of the Presbyterian church in Ripley. Harriet undoubtedly heard many of the stories about fugitives and the UGRR from the Rankins, which gave context to her book *Uncle Tom's Cabin*. Rankin stated that he assisted more than two thousand people through the UGRR. This home is now a historic site managed by the National Park Service. After the war, Rankin and Jean continued to work for the church, and John preached at various churches in the north and central states while visiting with their children.

The National Underground Railroad Freedom Center in Cincinnati produced the film *Brothers of the Borderland*, which highlights the activities of John Parker's and John Rankin's families working together to help a fugitive escape. The film is shown in an experiential theater with background sounds and sights of the Ohio River as the plot takes place.

SCENIC BYWAYS

Kentucky Side

Route 8 is a scenic byway designation on the road that courses along the highway between Augusta to Maysville, Kentucky.

The Old Maysville-Lexington Turnpike (Paris Pike) from Maysville to Lexington is one of the most beautiful scenic byways that bisects the famous bluegrass region thoroughbred racehorse farms.

Ohio Side

The Ohio River Scenic Byway continues its route through Cincinnati, Richmond, Chilo Lock 34, Point Pleasant and Ripley. http://www.ohioscenicbyway/com/maps.

PLACES TO VISIT

OHIO SIDE

Clermont County

Chilo Lock 34 Park and Museum

The Chilo Lock 34 Visitor Center and Museum occupies the former operation of Ohio River Lock Dam No. 34, which was decommissioned by the Army Corps of Engineers in 1964. Living and Working with the Ohio River is the theme of interactive exhibits and displays to learn more about the history of the Ohio River. It is a great place for a stop to relax and enjoy the river. There is also a playground and the Crooked Run Nature Preserve on the thirty-eight acres. There are several annual events including Steamboat Days in August.

Website: www.clermontparks.org
Address: 521 County Park Road, Chilo, Ohio
Phone: (513) 876-9013.

US Grant Birthplace

This frontier cottage on the Ohio River is the birthplace of Ulysses S. Grant, who some say did more for blacks than Abraham Lincoln.[108] It was Grant who was responsible for the passing of Fifteenth Amendment, which gave blacks the right to vote. He also signed legislation to limit activities of the Ku Klux Klan and at times stationed federal troops throughout the South to maintain law and order. Grant attended academies in both Maysville and Ripley, Ohio (the Ripley Academy was under the leadership of abolitionist John Rankin). Grant's father was apprenticed as a tanner under Owen Brown, father of radical abolitionist John Brown

150

Clio Lock no. 34 Park is a museum dedicated to the history of locks created on the Ohio River by the Army Corps of Engineers. *Author's collection*.

President Ulysses Grant's birthplace is commemorated in this modest home along the Ohio River. Daily tours interpret Grant's family and their stance against slavery. *Author's collection*.

of Harpers Ferry. There is a small river park across the street from the US Grant Birthplace.

Website: www.usgrantbirthplace.org
Address: 1551 State Run 232, Point Pleasant, Ohio
Phone: (800) 283-8932

Brown County

Ripley

Revolutionary War soldier Colonel Poage founded this town in 1804 on the Ohio River. He originally called it Staunton. A Virginian by birth, Poage was staunchly opposed to slavery and others, such as fellow Virginian senator Dr. Alexander Campbell, followed his lead. These abolitionists attracted others, and soon one of those, Presbyterian minister John Rankin, had a house on the ridge with a light that became a beacon for freedom seekers. John Parker soon joined the ranks of Ripley abolitionists and placed his home at the river's edge. All working in tandem with one another, the Ripley abolitionists became a well-known force against advancing bounty hunters and slaveholders looking for fugitives.

Today the town is well preserved with nineteenth-century businesses and homes lining the waterfront. There is a trail at the John Parker historic site on the river and a waterfront walkway with historic markers. A walk through the Parker site and a drive up the steep embankment to the Rankin house puts you in back in place and time.

John Parker House

This is a beautifully preserved acre that commemorates Parker's foundry work and courage as a conductor on the Underground Railroad. The location of Parker's on the waterfront attests to the danger and risk that Parker and his family were exposed to everyday in helping fugitives. During the Civil War, Parker was a key recruiter for the Twenty-Seventh Ohio Volunteer Infantry Colored Regiment. He was a successful inventor with three patents to his credit (see tobacco press at the Harriet Beecher Stowe Museum in Washington, Kentucky). He and his family were very involved in the UGRR. There is a path with interpretive signage on

UGRR conductor John Parker's house and iron foundry business is a national historic landmark on the waterfront at Ripley. *Author's collection.*

Parker's family and life. Hours are seasonal so call ahead to make sure they are open.

Address: 300 North Front Street, Ripley, Ohio
Phone: (937) 392-4044 or (937) 92-4188. 45167.

John Rankin House
John Rankin's Presbyterian church is at the bottom of the steep steps in downtown Ripley that lead up to the Rankin house. The staircase is currently in disrepair with plans to fix it in the future. The Rankin House is now a part of the National Park Service, and there is a great interpretive center on the ridge behind the Rankin home with restrooms and a gift shop. The road leading up to the site is steep and curvy but is suitable for large tour buses and groups. Park service guides lead daily tours of the Rankin home. The hours are seasonal so call ahead to make sure they are open.

Address: 6152 Rankin Hill Road, Ripley, Ohio
Phone: (937) 392-4044. 45167.

Above: UGRR conductor John Rankin's house and museum operated by the National Park Service stands as a beacon of freedom on the high ridge at Ripley. *Author's collection.*

Left: The Presbyterian church in Ripley was John Rankin's church and the center for antislavery meetings. *Author's collection.*

KENTUCKY SIDE

Augusta, Bracken County

Augusta is a beautiful, quaint town with a row of historic homes that line the riverfront and an operating ferry that takes cars back and forth from the Ohio to Kentucky shore, each day. This is one of the last active ferry crossings on the Ohio River. The town's charter was issued on October 7, 1797. The town was developed on top of a Native American burial site with an estimated ten thousand remains still buried there.

The town was very busy during the antebellum years with centers of learning such as Augusta College and Bracken Academy. Both of these schools were learning centers for abolitionists, such as John G. Fee and James Thome. There are several homes that served as safehouses on the UGRR.

On September 27, 1862, Colonel Basil Duke of the Confederate army had plans to disperse a Union militia of 125 men led by Colonel Joshua Bradford. Residents of Augusta, along with the Union soldiers, fought the rebel soldiers in hand-to-hand combat, causing Duke to abandon his plans to take the war onto Northern soil.

Website: www.battleofaugusta.com

Augusta Seminary

Augusta College was founded by the Ohio and Kentucky Methodist Church Conference in 1822 and was known for debates on slavery. Abolitionists such as John Gregory Fee and Thome attended the college. There were antislavery debates held here that included Henry Rucker, who spoke against federal laws that gave rights to own another human being. Today, the Augusta Public School building sits on the site of the former college. The dormitory, located directly across the street, still stands and is undergoing renovation efforts by the Augusta Historical Society.[109]

August Waterfront

The August waterfront has a special charm and one of the very few nineteenth-century waterfronts left in the country. Buildings vary from pioneer, federal and Victorian. The brickhouse at 209 West Riverside is one of the oldest in northern Kentucky. The building at the corner of

The Augusta Seminary dormitory is currently under restoration by the Bracken County Historical Society. *Author's collection.*

The ferry at Augusta has operated since 1798, providing daily service between Augusta and Boudes Landing on US 52 in Ohio. *Author's collection.*

Riverside and Main Streets was a drugstore and was hit by Morgan's Raiders in the 1862 Confederate attack. It now houses the Beehive Restaurant, which serves regional specialties. Augusta's walking tour map lists fifty-four buildings, including a waterfront house owned by singer Rosemary Clooney, a native of Maysville. A map can be obtained at the tourism center at the Red Trolley on the waterfront.

The Old Jail in Augusta

Thought to be the oldest extant jail in Kentucky, built in 1811, it was part of the Augusta town square where the original courthouse was built in the early 1800s. The courthouse burned in 1848. Inside of the brick structure is a smaller log building that held the incarcerated. Slaves accused of criminal acts were held in the dungeon of this jail.[110] The jail sits in the center of the town, slightly on a hill.

The Augusta jail is the oldest extant jail in Kentucky and often helped fugitive slaves and UGRR conductors such as John Fairfield. *Author's collection.*

Methodist Episcopal Church

This church in Augusta was attended by John G. Fee and James Armstrong Thome when they were students at Augusta College. The Methodist Episcopal church was split over the issue of slavery and divided into northern and southern wings. This church is located on Riverside Drive and is now a residence.

The Methodist Episcopal church in Augusta was attended by John Fee and the Thome family. *Author's collection.*

Regina Lang and Carolyn Miller

Regina Lang is the manager of Freedom Tyne Legacy and coordinates UGRR tours for groups of twenty-five or more through Mason County and neighboring Ohio. Her grandfather, Issac Lang, was a sharecropper on the former John W. Anderson farm near Germantown, Kentucky. His recollections of the property when he worked there as a youth, helped historians and researchers with the history of the Anderson Slave Jail that was reconstructed as a centerpiece exhibit in the Freedom Center in Cincinnati. Caroline Miller has provided important research on slave history for the region. Her book *Grape Vine Dispatch* is one of the most thorough sources on slave history in the region.

Baker-Bird Winery

Baker-Bird Winery, located outside of Augusta, is the oldest commercial winery in America. The land was purchased in 1811 by Abraham Baker Sr., and it was his son, John Baker Jr., who turned the region into a major wine-producing area. It is one of twenty-two wineries on the National Register

Regina Lang's grandfather provided oral histories regarding the Anderson Slave Jail. Caroline Miller is an expert on slave history and the UGRR. *Author's collection*.

The Baker-Bird Winery outside Augusta is the oldest commercial winery in America. *Author's collection*.

of Historic Places. The winery was built from hand-cut blocks of limestone by German immigrants in an arched cellar that measured ninety feet long, forty feet high and forty feet wide. During a Civil War battle in August, it was used as a safehouse for families.

Address: 4465 Augusta Chatham Road, Augusta, Kentucky

Maysville, Mason County

Maysville, originally named Limestone, was established in 1787 because of a landing cut by migrating buffalo that were traveling across the river to the Blue Licks in Kentucky for salt. Maysville became the major passageway into the interior of Kentucky, as well as points south and west. There are 155 buildings in Maysville listed on the National Register of Historic Places. Some of the buildings are terraced on the hillside that overlooks this charming river town. When the Marquis de Lafayette made his famous visit across the United States in 1825, Maysville red carpets covered the grade from Fish Street to Front Street. Robert Dafford historic murals (similar to the Dafford Murals in Covington) are painted at the floodwalls that depict the connection of the Ohio River to Maysville and four centuries of history, agriculture, the four seasons and various modes of transportation. The Mason County Courthouse, built in 1848, towers over the city. The original clock, with wooden gears installed in 1850, is said to be older than London's Big Ben clock and it was moved to the Kentucky Gateway Museum Clock Tower in 2007. The courthouse was the site of slave auctions.

Kentucky Gateway Museum

With more than four thousand regional artifacts, the museum highlights the regional history of the area with special displays on steamboat history, slavery and pioneer life. It also includes a beautiful diorama of river life in antebellum Maysville. Part of the building (circa 1878) served as the Maysville and Mason County Library. The museum has acquired the Kathleen Savage Browning Miniatures Collection—perhaps one of the most extensive collections of one-twelfth scale reproductions of homes, furnishings, clothing, artwork and people. The collections are constantly changing and being added with miniature dioramas of local landmarks and

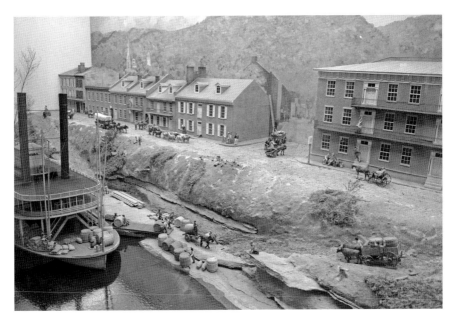

This diorama from the Kentucky Gateway Museum in Maysville depicts the wharf area in Maysville at the escape site of the Hayden family, who were assisted by Webster and Fairbank. *Author's collection.*

themed movies, such as Harry Potter. Victorian mansions, castles and much more are featured in these amazing miniature displays. The museum also includes a very well-organized archive and library with good sources on African American families, genealogical sources and history.

The museum has recently added the Old Pogue Experience—a downtown extension of the Old Pogue Distillery, offering a deeper look into bourbon and Pogue history in the birthplace of bourbon. On the other side of the museum is Phillip's Folly (227 Sutton Street), which was begun by William B. Phillips. Phillips was Maysville's second mayor, and he ran out of money during construction and disappeared, leading to the name "Phillip's Folly." John Armstrong bought the house in 1838. According to oral tradition, fugitive slaves were held in a wooden cell on the lower level of the house, and it became known as a stop on the UGRR. Open Tuesday through Saturday from 10:00 a.m. through 4:00 p.m. and closed Sunday and Monday. There is an admission charge.

Website: www.kygmc.org
Address: 215 Sutton Street, Maysville, Kentucky
Phone: (606) 564-5865

These stained-glass features mark the site of the black Baptist church formed by Elisha Green in Maysville. *Author's collection.*

Elisha Green and the Black Baptist Church

Born into slavery in Bourbon County, Elisha Green grew up in Mason County at Glen Alice farm outside Maysville. He later purchased freedom for himself and part of his family. A spiritual leader, he helped form African American churches in Maysville and Paris, Kentucky, and preached to many black congregations. Believing freedmen should own land, Green and a white landowner founded an African American community near Paris. He was chosen as vice-president of the Kentucky Negro Republican Party in Lexington in 1867. He remained a dynamic community leader throughout his life. He died in 1889. The marker is located at the intersection of Maddox Alley and West Fourth Street in Maysville.

Washington

Washington was incorporated in 1786 and grew to become a thriving town, second only to Lexington. It was the county seat until 1848 when it moved to Maysville. It had the first post office and first public waterworks system west of the Allegheny Mountains. Frontiersmen Simon Kenton and Thomas Williams arrived in Washington in 1775, discovering the rich cane lands. Kenton established his station here and began recruiting families and individuals to the area. Pioneer stations resembling military forts with blockhouses overlooking the compound that were built to protect against Indian attacks between 1775 and 1795, which were known as the Twenty Years' War. The seven-hundred-acre town of Washington was laid out in 1785 by Arthur Fox Sr. and William Wood. The town quickly grew from pioneer log cabins to sophisticated brick homes within a twenty-year period. Slave ownership and slave auctions were common in Washington leading into the 1850s. At this time, slave auctions were considered by some as a form of entertainment. This is where Harriet Beecher Stowe personally witnessed a slave auction. For tours and information contact Washington Visitors Center located at Paxton-Evans House.

Address: 2028 Old Main Street, Maysville, Kentucky
Phone: (606) 759-7411

George Morton III Home

Thorton Blackburn was three years old when he was purchased as a "gift" to nine-year old George Morton III at this house at 2014 Old Main Street. He lived here until 1826 when he was sold at age eleven to slaveholders in Louisville. The back section of this house has a marker that says Murphy Lashbrooke Home 1805. It was built by William Murphy, local postmaster, and is the site of Washington's first printing press. (See Blackburn Case in Louisville section).

Francis Taylor House

Francis Taylor was a slaveholder of the James Lightfoot family. James escaped to Canada and convinced Josiah Henson to go to Mason County and rescue the rest of the Lightfoot family. Even though Henson had a price on his head as a fugitive, he went down to Mason County and helped rescue members of the family.

Address: 2003-2005 Old Main Street, Washington, Kentucky

This tobacco press at the Harriet Beecher Stowe Museum in Washington was a patent by UGRR conductor John Parker. *Author's collection.*

Harriet Beecher Stowe Museum (formerly the Marshal Key home)

The Harriet Beecher Stowe Museum is the historic home of Marshal Key, a slave owner. He was clerk of the Mason County Court from 1814 until 1840. As clerk, one of his responsibilities was to host slave auctions at the nearby courthouse (no longer extant). Harriet Beecher Stowe visited the Keys, and the slave auction scene in *Uncle Tom's Cabin* was set at the courthouse in Washington. There are tours by appointment

Address: 2124 Old Main Street, P.O. Box 184, Washington, Kentucky
Phone: (606) 759-7411 (summer) or (606) 654-0250 (fall, winter and spring)

Germantown

A small community in Mason County, the Anderson farm is located nearby, where John Anderson's Slave Jail was deconstructed and moved to the Freedom Center Museum in Cincinnati. It is the same vicinity of the John and Matilda Fee farm, as well as Arnold Gragston (1840–1938). Gragston was a slave on the Tabb farm. He rowed many to freedom from Dover across the Ohio River. He eventually escaped with his family to Detroit. Because of Gragston's longevity, he was interviewed many times about his experiences as a conductor on the UGRR. His stories were included in an HBO documentary in 2003 called *Unchained Memories*. A historical marker is dedicated to both John Fee and Arnold Gragston in Germantown.

NOTES

Introduction

1. Robinson, *History of Navigation*, 9.
2. Ibid., 4.
3. Guasco, "Misguided Focus."
4. Dattel, "Cotton in the Global Economy."
5. Coleman, *Slavery Times in Kentucky*, 131–41.
6. Townsend, *Lincoln and the Bluegrass*.
7. Trotter, *River Jordan*, 28.
8. Greenburg, *Nat Turner*.
9. Sherwood, "Formation of the American Colonization Society."
10. Cooper, "Doing Battle," 125.
11. Hudson, *Fugitive Slaves*; Peters, *Underground Railroad in Floyd County, Indiana*; Gibson, *Historical Sketch of the Progress of the Colored Race*.
12. Collins, *Historical Sketches of Kentucky*, 131.
13. Bibb, *Life and Adventures*, p. 47.
14. Siebert, *Underground Railroad from Slavery to Freedom*, 78–79.
15. Ibid., 144.
16. Peters, *Underground Railroad in Floyd County, Indiana*, 121–22.
17. Siebert, *Underground Railroad from Slavery to Freedom*, 142.
18. Ibid., 146.
19. Lammlein, *History and Families*, 54.
20. Siebert, *Underground Railroad from Slavery to Freedom*, 312.
21. Ibid., 82–83.
22. Oldham County Historical Society Archives, 1824 Circuit Court Case, Lucy, Woman of Color.

Chapter 1

23. Nunes, "Salt Licks and Slavery."
24. Bartelt, *There I Grew Up*, 58.
25. Hudson, *Fugitive Slaves*.

Chapter 2

26. Lucas, *History of Blacks in Kentucky*.
27. Robinson, *History of Navigation*, 7.
28. Ibid., 8.
29. *Louisville Daily Courier*, July 3, 1860, 2.
30. Robinson, *History of Navigation*, 106.
31. Ibid., 102.
32. Coffin, *Reminiscences of Levi Coffin*, 265.
33. Collins, *Historical Sketches of Kentucky*, 152.
34. Blassingame, "Slave Testimony," 385–86.
35. Siebert, *Underground Railroad from Slavery to Freedom*, 151.
36. Runyon, *Delia Webster*, 151–52.
37. Blassingame, "Slave Testimony," 386.
38. Hudson, *Fugitive Slaves*, 120.
39. Ibid., 109.
40. Peters, *Underground Railroad in Floyd County, Indiana*.
41. Frost, *I've Got a Home*.
42. Hudson, *Fugitive Slaves*, 111.
43. Peters, *Underground Railroad in Floyd County, Indiana*.
44. Goodall, *Works Progress Administration*, 50.
45. Ibid., 312–13.
46. Coffin, *Reminiscences of Levi Coffin*, 267.
47. Peters, *Underground Railroad in Floyd County, Indiana*.
48. Karem, *Exploring the Zachary Taylor National Cemetery*.

Chapter 3

49. Runyon, *Delia Webster*, 126.
50. Ibid.
51. Lammlein, *History and Families*, 54.

52. Coon, *Southeastern Indiana's Underground Railroad*.

53. Hudson, *Fugitive Slaves*, 15.

54. "Underground Railroad Sites in Indiana," Indiana Historical Board, Indiana Department of Natural Resources, accessed May 13, 2019, http://IN.gov.

55. Historic Madison, *Madison Indiana, 1854 Section 8*.

56. Fairbank, *During Slavery Times*, 57.

57. Coon, *History by Perrine*.

58. Cooper, *Doing Battle*, 86.

59. Ibid., 70.

60. Coleman, *Slavery Times in Kentucky*, 242–43.

61. Cooper, *Doing Battle*, 227.

62. Ibid., 461.

63. Ibid., 477.

64. Runyon, *Delia Webster*, 3.

65. Fairbank, *During Slavery Times*, 57.

66. Runyon, *Delia Webster*.

67. Interview by Nancy Theiss with Pam Venard, January 2019.

68. Oldham County Historical Society. The Oldham County Historical Society has county court records that date to the county's creation in 1824. Other documents include family papers, images and maps that span two hundred years.

69. James and Amanda Mount Collection donated by Lucretia Davenport (2004), Oldham County Historical Society.

70. Rewell, *Men of Mark*.

71. "Phillip Telfair Henshaw," Geni, accessed June 2, 2019, http://www.geni.com.

72. Sanders Family Letters Collection, Drew County Historical Society.

73. Coon, *Southeastern Indiana's Underground Railroad*, 70.

Chapter 4

74. Taylor, *Frontiers of Freedom*, 36–7.

75. Siebert, *Underground Railroad from Slavery to Freedom*, 119.

76. Lucas, *History of Blacks in Kentucky*, 67.

77. Siebert, *Underground Railroad from Slavery to Freedom*, 97.

78. Miller, *Grape Vine Disatch*, 52.

79. Ibid., 171–75.

80. Goodall, *Works Progress Administration*, 138–39.
81. Siebert, *Underground Railroad from Slavery to Freedom*, 119.
82. Coffin, *Reminiscences of Levi Coffin*, 159.
83. Ibid., 337–45.
84. Coffin, *Reminiscences of Levi Coffin*, 286.
85. Ibid., 293.
86. Smiddy and Porter, "Escape of the 28."
87. Ibid., 3.
88. Coffin, *Reminiscences of Levi Coffin*, 151–56.
89. Haviland, *Woman's Life-Work*, 171–303.
90. "Gilbert Van Zandt," Ohio History Connection, Ohio History Central, accessed May 2, 2019, http://ohiohistorycentral.org.

Chapter 5

91. Runyon, *Delia Webster*, 16.
92. Henderson and O'Malley, "Ribbon of History."
93. Coleman, *Slavery Times in Kentucky*, 138–41.
94. Miller, *Shackles, Iron Bars*.
95. For more on slave traders, see Coleman, *Slavery Times in Kentucky*; Miller, *Grape Vine Dispatch*; Siebert, *Underground Railroad from Slavery to Freedom*.
96. Harriet Beecher Stowe Museum, Washington, Kentucky.
97. Miller, *Grape Vine Dispatch*, 186.
98. Sprague, *His Promised Land*, 125
99. Miller, *Grape Vine Dispatch*, 168–75.
100. Ibid., 173–75.
101. Ibid., 27–30.
102. Fee, *Autobiography of John G. Fee*.
103. Miller, *Grape Vine Dispatch*.
104. Miller, *Juliet Miles*, 250–54.
105. Hagedorn, *Beyond the River*, 12–13.
106. Sprague, *His Promised Land*, 136.
107. Ibid., 137–38.
108. Chernow, *Grant*.
109. Miller, *Juliet Miles*.
110. Miller, *Grape Vine Dispatch*, 129.

BIBLIOGRAPHY

Ambler, Charles Henry. *A History of Transportation in the Ohio Valley*. Glendale, CA: Arthur H. Clark Company, 1932.

Anderson, William J. *Life and Narrative of William J. Anderson: Twenty-Four Years a Slave; Sold Eight Times! In Jail Sixty Times! Whipped Three Hundred Times!!!* Chicago: Daily Tribune Book and Job Printing Office, 1857. Reprint, Chapel Hill, NC: Academic Affairs Library, 2000.

Bartelt, William, E. *There I Grew Up: Remember Abraham Lincoln's Indiana Youth.* Indianapolis: Indiana Historical Society, 2008.

Bibb, Henry. *The Life and Adventures of Henry Bibb: An American Slave.* N.p., 1849. Reprinted with introduction by Charles Heglar. Madison: University Press of Wisconsin, 2001

Blassingame, John W. "Slave Testimony: Samuel G. Howe Interview of Washington Spradling, 1863." From American Freedman's Inquiry Commission Interviews, 1977.

Blockson, Charles L. *Hippocrene Guide to the Underground Railroad*. New York: Hippocrene Books, 1995.

Chernow, Ron. *Grant*. New York: Penguin Books, 2018.

Coffin, Levi. *Reminiscences of Levi Coffin*. Abridged and edited by Ben Richmond. Richmond, IN: Friends United Press, 2006.

Coleman, J. Winston, Jr. *Slavery Times in Kentucky.* Chapel Hill: University of North Carolina Press, 1940.

Collins, Lewis. *Historical Sketches of Kentucky: Its History, Antiquities, and Natural Curiosities, Geographical, Statistical and Geological Descriptions; with Anecdotes of*

Pioneer Life, and More Than One Hundred Biographical Sketches of Distinguished Pioneers, Soldier, Statesmen, Jurists, Lawyers, Divines, etc. Cincinnati: Lewis Collins and J.A. and U.P. James, 1850.

Coon, Diane Perrine. *History by Perrine* (blog). Accessed June 30, 2019: http://www.historybyperrine.com. Website with posts by Diane Coon contain research and information on the Underground Railroad from her last twenty years in the region.

————. *Southeastern Indiana's Underground Railroad Routes and Operations.* Indiana Department of Natural Resources, Division of Historic Preservation and Archaeology, U.S. Department of Interior, National Park Service, 2001.

Cooper, Afua. "Doing Battle in Freedom's Cause: Henry Bibb, Abolitionism, Race Uplift and Black Manhood, 1842–1854." Diss., University of Toronto, 2000.

Cramer, Zodak. *The Navigator: Containing Directors for Navigating the Monongahela, Allegheny, Ohio and Mississippi River.* Pittsburgh: Cramer and Spear, 1821.

Dattel, Eugene R. *Cotton and Race in the Making of America: The Human Costs of Economic Power.* New York: Ivan R. Dee, 2009.

————. "Cotton in the Global Economy." Mississippi History Now. Mississippi Historical Society. Accessed June 21, 2019. http://mshistorynow.mdah.state.ms.us.

DuFour, John James. *The American Vine-Dresser's Guide: Being a Treatise on the Cultivation of the Vine and the Process of Wine Making Adapted to the Soil and Climate of the United States.* Cincinnati: S.J. Browne, 1826. Reprint, Vevay, IN: Switzerland County Historical Society, 1999.

Exploring a Common Past: Researching and Interpreting the Underground Railroad. 3rd ed. Washington, D.C.: National Park Service, 2000.

Fairbank, Reverend Calvin. *During Slavery Times: How He Fought the Good Fight to Prepare the Way.* Chicago: R.R. McCabe, 1890.

Fee, John G. *Autobiography of John G. Fee.* Chapel Hill, NC: Academic Affairs Library, 1997.

Field, T.P. *Kentucky and the Southwest Territory.* 1794. Map.

Frost, Karolyn Smardz. *I've Got a Home in Gloryland: A Lost Tale of the Underground Railroad.* New York: Farrat, Strauss and Giroux, 2007.

Gibson, W.H., Sr. *Historical Sketch of the Progress of the Colored Race in Louisville, Ky., as Noted by the Writer During a Period of Fifty Years.* Louisville, KY: Bradley and Gilbert Company, 1897.

————. *History of the United Brothers of Friendship and Sisters of the Mysterious Ten, a Negro Order Organized August 1, 1861 in the City of Louisville, Ky.* Louisville, KY: Bradley and Gilbert Company, 1897.

Gilleland, J.C. *The Ohio and Mississippi Pilot*. N.p.: Palala Press, 1820.

Goodall, Hurley. *Works Progress Administration Writers Project: Underground Railroad: The Invisible Road to Freedom Through Indiana*. Indianapolis, IN: DNR-DHPA, 2001.

Greenburg, Kenneth. *Nat Turner: A Slave Rebellion in History and Memory*. London: Oxford University Press, 2004.

Griffler, Keith P. *Frontline of Freedom: African Americans and the Forging of the Underground Railroad in the Ohio Valley*. Lexington: University of Kentucky Press, 2004.

Guasco, Michael. "The Misguided Focus on 1619 as the Beginning of Slavery in the U.S. Damages Our Understanding of American History." *Smithsonian*, September 13, 2017. https://www.smithsonianmag.com.

Hagedorn, Ann. *Beyond the River: The Untold Story of the Heroes of the Underground Railroad*. New York: Simon and Schuster, 2002.

Haviland, Laura S. *A Woman's Life-Work*. N.p. 1881. Reprint, Fairford, Gloucester, England: Echo Library, 2012.

Henderson, Gywnn, and Nancy O'Malley. "Ribbon of History—The Maysville to Lexington Road." *Kentucky Heritage Spotlight* (publication). Preservation Kentucky. Kentucky Heritage Council. July 24, 2018. http://preservationkentucky.org.

Historic Madison. *Madison, Indiana, 1854 Section 8 Georgetown Historical Interpretive Walking Tour*. Madison, IN: Historic Madison, 2008.

Horowitz, Tony. *Midnight Rising: John Brown and the Raid that Sparked the Civil War*. New York: Henry Holt, 2011.

Hudson, J. Blaine. *Fugitive Slaves and the Underground Railroad in the Kentucky Borderland*. Jefferson, NC: McFarland and Company, 2002.

Johnson, Leland R. "Engineering the Ohio." In *Always a River: The Ohio River and the American Experience*. Edited by Robert L. Reid. Bloomington: Indiana University Press, 1991.

Karem, Kenny. *Exploring the Zachary Taylor National Cemetery and the Monuments of President Taylor and the Military Veterans: An Illustrated Activity Guidebook for Zachary Taylor National Cemetery*. Self-published, 2017. Kindle.

Lammlein, Dorothy C., et al., eds. *History and Families of Oldham County Kentucky: The First Century 1824–1924*. Paducah: Turner Publishing, 1996.

Lucas, Marion B. *A History of Blacks in Kentucky: From Slavery to Segregation, 1760–1891*. 2nd ed. Frankfort: Kentucky Historical Society, 2017.

Marrs, Reverend Elijah P. *Life and History of the Rev. Elijah P. Marrs*. Louisville, KY: Beargrass Baptist Church, 1885. Reprinted 1979.

Miller, Caroline R. *Grape Vine Dispatch: The Voice of Antislavery Messages.* Brooksville, KY: Bracken County Historical Society, 2011.

———. *Juliet Miles and Matilda Fee's Anti-Slavery Crusade.* Historical Reflections 11. Brooksville, KY: Bracken County Historical Society, 2008.

———. *Shackles, Iron Bars, and Coffle Chains: Devices Utilized by Slave Trader John W. Anderson.* Historical Reflections 12. Brooksville, KY: Bracken County Historical Society, 2008.

Morrison, Toni. *Beloved.* New York: Alfred A. Knopf, 1987.

Myer, William Edward. *Indian Trails of the Southeast.* Nashville, TN: Blue and Gray Press, 1971.

Notable Kentucky African American Database. University of Kentucky Libraries Special Collections Research Center. Accessed June 30, 2019. http://www.nkaa.uky.edu. Ongoing website with more than two hundred biographical entries on African Americans in and from the state of Kentucky.

Nunes, Bill. "Salt Licks and Slavery in Illinois." *St. Louis Post-Dispatch.* October 17, 2007. http://www.stiltoday.com.

Oldham County Historical Society Archives, 1824 Circuit Court Case, Lucy, Woman of Color.

Pearce, John, ed. *The Ohio River.* Lexington: University of Kentucky Press. 1989.

Peters, Pamela R. *The Underground Railroad in Floyd County, Indiana.* Jefferson, NC: McFarland, 2001.

Powell, Jim. *The Triumph of Liberty.* New York: Free Press, 2000.

Raitz, Karl, and Nancy O'Malley. *Kentucky's Frontier Highway: Historical Landscapes along the Maysville Road.* Lexington: University of Kentucky Press, 2012.

Rankin, John. *Letters on American Slavery: Addressed to Mr. Thomas Rankin.* Boston: Garrison and Knapp, 1833.

Rewell, George M. *Men of Mark.* Cleveland, OH: Geo. M. Ewell and Company, 1887.

Reynolds, David S. *John Brown, Abolitionist: The Man Who Killed Slavery, Sparked the Civil War and Seeded Civil Rights.* New York: Vintage Books, 2006.

Robinson, Michael C. *History of Navigation in the Ohio River Basin.* Washington, D.C.: National Waterways Study, U.S. Army Engineer Water Resources Support Center, 1983.

Runyon, Randolph Paul. *Delia Webster and the Underground Railroad.* Lexington: University of Kentucky Press, 1996.

Salafia, Mathew. *Slavery's Borderland: Freedom and Bondage along the Ohio River.* Philadelphia, PA: University of Philadelphia Press, 2013.

Sanders Family Letters Collection. Drew County Historical Society.

Sherwood, Henry Noble. "The Formation of the American Colonization Society." *Journal of Negro History* 2 no. 3 (1917): 209–28.

Siebert, Wilbur H. *The Underground Railroad from Slavery to Freedom: A Comprehensive History.* Mineola, NY: Dover, 2006.

Smiddy, Betty Ann, and Porter, Diane. (nd). "The Escape of the 28." Hamilton Avenue Road to Freedom. December 23, 2013. http://hamiltonavenueroadtofreedom.org.

Sprague, Stuart Seely, ed. *His Promised Land: The Autobiography of John Parker, Former Slave and Conductor on the Underground Railroad.* New York: W. W. Norton, 1996.

Stowe, Harriet Beecher. *A Key to Uncle Tom's Cabin: Presenting the Original Facts and Documents upon Which the Story is Founded.* Leipzig: Bernhard Tauchnitz, 1853. Google Books.

———. *Uncle Tom's Cabin.* Signet Classics ed. New York: Signet, 2008.

Taylor, Nikki M. *Frontiers of Freedom: Cincinnati's Black Community, 1802–1868.* Athens: University of Ohio Press, 2005.

Theiss, Nancy Stearns. *Life at the River's Edge.* Charleston, SC: The History Press, 2010.

Toler, Herbert H., Jr. "Nothin' but 'ligion: The American Missionary Association's Activities in the Nation's Capital, 1852–1875." PhD diss., Columbia University, 2014.

Toqueville, Alexis de. *Democracy in America and Two Essays on America.* Penguin Classics ed. New York: Penguin, 2003.

Townsend, William. *Lincoln and the Bluegrass: Slavery and Civil War in Kentucky.* Lexington: University of Kentucky Press, 1955.

Trotter, Joe William, Jr. *River Jordan: African American Urban Life in the Ohio Valley.* Lexington: University of Kentucky Press, 1998.

Way, Frederick, Jr. *Way's Packet Directory 1848–1983: Passenger Steamboats of the Mississippi River System since the Advent of Photography in Mid-Continent America.* Athens: University of Ohio Press, 1983.

Webster, Delia Ann. *Kentucky Jurisprudence: A History of the Trial of Miss Delia A. Webster at Lexington, Kentucky, Dec. 17–21, 1844 before the Hon. Richard Buckner; on a Charge of Aiding Slaves to Escape from that Commonwealth—with Miscellaneous Remarks Including Her View on American Slavery, 1845.* Cornell University Library Digital Collections.

Wilhelm, Paul, Duke of Wurttemburg. *Travels in North America, 1822–1824.* Reprint. Norman: University of Oklahoma Press, 1973.

Woods, Dylan, ed. "John Finley Crowe." *Hanover Historical Review* 11 (2010).

ABOUT THE AUTHOR

Nancy is a native of Oldham County, where she grew up on the family farm and married her childhood sweetheart. She has degrees in education, biology and environmental studies. She has taught in the public school system, worked for the Kentucky Department of Education and the Kentucky Department of Fish and Wildlife. She has been director of several nonprofits and currently works as the executive director of the Oldham County Historical Society. She has written history columns for the *Louisville Courier-Journal* and the *Oldham Era*, as well as articles and books. She has received many recognitions for her various endeavors. An avid naturalist and historian, Nancy believes that knowing your community and the people, places and living things (past and present) around you, gives you an understanding of your importance and place in the world.